Shift Thinking™
40 Key Principles to Rewire Your Mind
and Skyrocket Your Sales

The material in this book is designed to provide general information about the subject matter covered. Use is granted with the understanding that the publisher and author are not engaged in rendering legal, financial or psychological advice. If expert assistance is required in these areas, the services of a competent professional should be sought.

The purpose of this information is to educate and entertain. The author and publisher shall have neither liability nor responsibility to any person or entity with respect to any loss or damage caused, or alleged to be caused, directly or indirectly, by the information contained herein.

Cover Design by Chris Sadowski at wildmoonstudios.net

To order additional copies of this book visit:

sellingskillsinstitute.com

amazon.com

Table of Contents

This book is dedicated to my three children - Brittany, Taylor and Dean. Always remember, you have within you the strength, the courage, and the passion to live the life you have always dreamed about. Dream BIG...reach for the stars.

You are the joy and happiness of my life. I am a very lucky man because of all of you. Being your Dad is my greatest reward.

I love you.
DAD

40 Key Principles to Rewire Your Mind and Skyrocket Your Sales

Charles Anderson, is the author of *The Secret to Sales Greatness, Opportunity Calling - The Easy Way to Double Your Number of New Qualified Appointments* and creator of the *Shift Thinking™ Sales Model*. In this practical and inspiring book, he turns to the principles he's studied, taught, and lived by for more than two decades.

These key principles will guide you through the process of rewiring your brain so you can be free of self-imposed limitations and finally become the success you were born to be.

In the last 50 years, salespeople have read millions of books, listened to thousands of hours of CD's, and heard hundreds of hours of sales training talks. So why do they struggle with the same sales problems today that they struggled with 50 years ago?

Because salespeople have been misinformed and not properly trained. They've been taught what to say, how to say it, and when to say it--but they haven't been taught how to recognize and overcome self-limiting thinking that rob them of the potential they were born with and stops them from achieving their best sales results.

Moving from being an average salesperson to being a sales champion does not require that you be a rocket scientist or brain surgeon. It requires no higher education, no advanced degrees in psychology or sociology. It does, however, require that you adjust your view of the world and create a clear vision of who you really are. And you can only have this clear vision when you wipe away the distortions caused by unhealthy thinking.

If you want to dramatically improve your sales results, you must not just change your actions, you must first change the meaning you assign to your thoughts --which is the essence of *Shift Thinking*.

With *Shift Thinking*, Charles Anderson introduces a set of principles that will help you work from the inside out to rewire your brain. Not merely a collection of good ideas, this book spells out 40 key principles, each one empowering you to break through self-imposed limitations, recondition negative thinking, eliminate unwanted behaviors, boost self-esteem, overcome fear, and live with passion and purpose.

Not long ago, it was thought that the brain you were born with was the brain you would die with. Your brain was thought to be "hard-wired" to function in predetermined ways. It turns out that's not true. Your brain is not hard-wired, it's "soft-wired" by external experiences and internal conditioning.

There are many things in your life that you cannot control, but you can control what really matters: your mind--and how it directs your thoughts, beliefs, and actions. Because we can notice and observe how our mind reacts, it means we actually have a choice in modifying our behavior.

An exciting result of the last 20 years of brain research is that as our brain gets rewired we can improve many aspects of our lives. In his widely-acclaimed book, *The Brain That Changes Itself: Stories of Personal Triumph from the Frontiers of Brain Science*, Norman Doidge M.D. states plainly that the brain has the capacity to rewire itself and/or form new neural pathways — if we do the work. Just like exercise, the work requires repetition to reinforce new learning.

The brain effects every aspect of sales. Whether we're talking about closing sales, telephone prospecting, negotiating, presenting, or simply establishing rapport, all the 'mechanics' of selling begin with a thought.

I'm often asked: "Why do salespeople fail?" The failure rate in sales isn't the result of salespeople not having the necessary selling skills, it's that they don't have the proper mindset. Success continues to be an inside job, a job that's won or lost in the mind.

This book will open your eyes to a whole new truth about success. You'll learn that to succeed in sales you have to think differently about yourself, how you sell and your potential.

In this book, *Shift Thinking* is presented in an engaging format set as a sales training program given to seasoned sales professionals. The principles and underlying concepts are explained in a lively narrative that will lead you through the steps needed to recondition your mind and build a sales career for yourself that's better than you ever imagined possible.

Prologue

The auditorium echoed with applause. Camera lights flashed across the front rows. My keynote speech to the crowd had capped the Las Vegas Power Up Your Sales Expo. Though I'd given this talk dozens of times--my audiences have included small companies and Fortune 500 corporations--my pulse still thumped with exhilaration.

It's 183 steps from the hotel elevator through the auditorium entrance and up to this stage. Takes two minutes to walk. But it had taken me 23 years to gain the wisdom, the right, to stand here and expect people to listen.

I gathered my notes from the lectern and climbed down the podium. I made my way through a gauntlet of well-wishers and emerged backstage.

A tall man in an elegant suit waited. He extended his hand and introduced himself, though I already knew who he was. Sherman Jackson, CEO of Palisade Global Mutual, one of the largest insurance firms in the eastern United States.

His large hand enveloped mine, and we shook.

"Great speech," he said. "Lots of wonderful insights. Very inspiring. But what really caught my attention was this point: *Shift Thinking*."

"What you heard was three decades of hard knocks distilled to 45 minutes and that one point."

Jackson grinned and nodded. "I'd like to discuss a proposal with you."

I agreed. He invited me to the hotel lounge where we ordered cocktails.

"You're probably aware," Jackson said, "that my company prides itself in maintaining one of the best sales teams in the industry. My people are experienced. Well educated. Very well trained. There isn't a reputable sales course or seminar we haven't tried. Still..." his voice lagged, "I thought we'd reached a plateau in what my team can accomplish. Until now."

"What is it you'd like me to do?"

"Come to New York and train my sales team. But I want more than a pep talk. I want your secrets."

"There are no secrets," I replied, "just an understanding that has taken me a long time to gain and appreciate. An understanding that taught me success is the result of learning 'how to *shift thinking.*'"

***

A month later, I arrived in Palisade Global Mutual's Manhattan headquarters. Jackson led me to a large training room, 37 stories above the busy streets of Manhattan and introduced me to his senior staff. Forty-six of his salespeople--a neatly dressed group of men and women--waited for me, no doubt wondering what I could teach them that they hadn't already tried.

After brief comments by Jackson, I addressed the room.

"My name is Charles Anderson, and Mr. Jackson invited me to New York to work with you. But I want you to know that I've already been paid – so frankly, now that I'm here in Manhattan, I can say whatever I want."

A slightly tense laugh rippled throughout the training room.

"Looking back, '*Shift Thinking*' seems like the logical outcome of my years as a sales trainer and performance coach, but it was a lesson that I almost died learning."

Several in the crowd grimaced.

"In 2009, a heart attack put me in the hospital. As I lay in bed recovering, I was overcome with remorse. Remorse for letting this episode happen to me and more importantly, remorse for missing my oldest daughter's college graduation. I worried about making it home. I'd never been known as a quitter but maintaining a positive outlook wasn't easy. Especially knowing that just six months earlier, my mother had died from a sudden heart attack at the age of 77.

"But that setback, as unfortunate as it appeared, had sown the seeds for my rebound. Those seeds sprouted when my cardiologist told me that despite my continued anguish, my post-attack tests looked normal.

"He said, 'There isn't anything I see that would cause the pain you're experiencing. Healing after a heart attack has a lot to do with your mind and how you think. Your mind and mental state can have a profound effect on the way the body responds after a heart attack. The mind and body are interconnected. When one is affected, the other suffers."

"I embraced his advice and decided it wasn't my time to die. After I shifted my thinking around, in four days I was back home and, two weeks later, at work training 75 insurance salespeople in Chicago. It took that heart attack and my doctor's words to turn me from a skeptic to a believer of this dictum: "'Thought is the greatest and most powerful force on earth. Thoughts drive our feelings, attitudes, and actions.'"

I reached into my briefcase and withdrew a copy of *The Inner Game of Tennis*. I described the book, the controversy it fomented when first published, and segued into, "The author Tim Gallwey took a lot of heat for saying that every game has an inner and an outer game. Like tennis, sales is a game. The inner game is mastering the internal forces that determine your success - your thoughts, feelings, attitude, and beliefs.

"The outer game is measured by how well salespeople perform and the number of sales they close."

A man in the center row raised his hand. "I'm results-oriented. It doesn't matter what I think as long as I get the job done."

"But are you doing your job as well as you can? For example, years ago, I was in a sales meeting at a large commercial printing company. The vice president of sales singled out one of his salespeople, a young guy named Michael. There wasn't anything extraordinary about him, yet he was their top earner, making $195,000 annually, more than double the company average of $77,000. What explained his success?"

I paced in front of the room. "Did he work harder or longer hours?" I looked at the salespeople and answered my question. "No."

I volleyed questions at them. "Did he have a better territory?

"Again, no.

"Better health? Better education? Better talent? No, Michael was as average as you could be...except for one thing."

I let the comment hang.

"The difference between Michael and the other salespeople, between his success and theirs, was that he thinks differently."

There was a furious scribbling of notes.

Jackson asked, "Explain what you mean by thinking differently."

"Simple," I replied. "I've studied successful salespeople for 23 years, and although the diversity you find among them is astounding, I've found that they are all alike in one way: how they think. The more I observed, the more salespeople I talked with, and the deeper I dug into their success, the clearer the answer. The salespeople who choose excellence over mediocrity think differently."

Several in the front row knit their brows, as if questioning my reasoning.

"That's why I'm here," I declared, "to help you break out of your 'success holding pattern' and move you to a new level of wealth, success, and happiness."

"To achieve greater success you must first win the inner-game of selling. To win the inner-game, you must think differently."

I invested the morning laying the foundation for my presentation and introduced the key principles of *shift thinking.*

Key Principle # 1

Break Through Self-Imposed Limitations

During the break, while I was getting a cold drink, I noticed one of the salesmen lingering close by. I got the sense he wanted to talk but not in front of the group. I led him down the hall to a spot beside an enormous window with a view of the Manhattan streets.

Once we had a bit of privacy, he mentioned his name, William Daniels, and launched into his concern. "I'm one of the firm's top performers, always in the upper ten percent. Yet I feel discouraged."

"Like something is holding you back?"

"Exactly," he replied.

"This leads to the first principle we had discussed in class. Break Through Self-imposed Limitations."

"But my lack of sales is the result of this bad economy. How can the economy be self-imposed?"

"Don't believe everything you think. What if I told you the economy had little to do with your performance? If your lack of performance was solely due to the economy, you would've implemented a plan of action. But you haven't because your obstacles are internal. These obstacles are the barriers that hold you back."

His big blue eyes seemed to drop to the floor, which prompted me to say, "Tell me more about your frustrations."

"I always feel pressed for time and feel like I have to choose between work and my family."

"That's a value conflict. What else? Maybe something from your past."

Daniels looked away and sighed. "My parents sacrificed a lot to get me through college. The plan was for me to become a lawyer. And here I am, a salesman."

"Meaning you feel guilty for disappointing them?"

"A bit."

"I bet that ties into a perception that your self-image doesn't measure up to your talents."

He grimaced like I'd stung him.

"What are your strengths?" I asked.

He thought for a moment. "I've always been organized. Disciplined. Competitive in sports, school, and here at work."

"And those talents come to you naturally?"

"I think they do."

"Then leverage them. Don't devalue them. A lot of folks," I motioned to the other salespeople by the coffee urns, "are undoubtedly envious of your talents. Those talents are your strengths. Play into them."

"Still," he said, "I feel like I'm coming up short."

"According to whom?"

"Me. I feel like I need to spend more time at home with my family. And I feel like I have to be the strong horse pulling my team's wagon."

"So, part of you wants to spend more time at home, while another part can't do enough at the office."

"You've nailed my situation. I want to do so much, but I can't be everywhere and can't do everything."

"That's a major internal barrier. Trapped between your desires and reality. That causes unclear priorities."

"There are. So, what do I do?"

The key step to overcoming your barriers is self-knowledge. Once you identify your internal and external barriers, you'll be in a better position to move beyond them.

Internal barriers include unhealthy thinking such as: fear, lack of confidence, self-deception, and self-limiting beliefs that prevent you from exploring new possibilities.

For instance, one person may not go for the job of her dreams because her fear of failure acts as an internal barrier. Another salesperson may avoid calling on C-level decision makers because he doesn't have the self-confidence to talk with 'important' people.

External barriers include people and the environment. Remember, you are a direct reflection of the people you associate with, as are your income, attitude, and lifestyle.

"What you can't do is to allow the naysayers and slackers to keep you stuck. There will be times of self-doubt and hesitation. When that happens, encourage yourself. Get motivated. Believe in yourself. You haven't come this far by accident. One thing is crystal clear--the outer condition of your career will always be in sync with your inner thinking."

"In sync," Daniels said. "How do I do that?"

"That's the second of the principles we discussed. Think Your Way to the Top."

Think Your Way to the Top

"Let me start by quoting Mohandas Gandhi. He said, 'A man is but the product of his thoughts: what he thinks, he becomes.'

"Thought is the greatest and most powerful force on earth. Thoughts control your life, mold your character and shape your sales career."

Daniels frowned skeptically.

I smiled at him. "The power of your mind is awesome. You can use your mind to achieve success that, until now, you have only dreamed of. It's a universal truth that life moves in the direction of your predominant thoughts.

"Whatever thoughts you have programmed into your head, or allowed others to program into your head, are controlling everything about you. While we can't fully control our lives, we can with the right interpretation of our thoughts, exert a huge influence on whether we fail or succeed. Are you familiar with Earl Nightingale?"

"Sure," Daniels replied, "I've listened to his motivational recordings."

"What about his most famous? *The Strangest Secret*. We become what we think about all day long." I explained, "Whatever you're doing, whatever you feel, whatever you want—all are determined by your thoughts. If your sales career isn't where you want it to be, then it's probably because your situation is tied to the way you think about yourself.

"If you are thinking that your situation is unique, people around you do not understand you, your goals are a little too far out of reach and the economy is holding you back, you're focused on the wrong problems. Maybe the real problem is your thinking."

Daniels responded with an abrupt, "What do you mean, maybe the real problem is my thinking?"

"I'm not following. You talk as if I'm not trying to succeed."

"I'm sure you are, but is that enough?

"Ask yourself this: If I don't adjust the meaning I assign to my thoughts and do things differently, how will I ever change my RESULTS? The blunt truth is you can't ... Without right thinking and right action there can be no right RESULT. This is the key behind all accomplishment, no matter how big or small.

"Very often a change in our point of view is needed more than a change of scenery. It is very easy to get stuck running down a tunnel that has no light at the end. Even though there is no light at the end of that tunnel, we keep running down that same tunnel because it has become our 'point of view' of how we do things."

I swept one hand across the city panorama beyond the window. "Keep in mind all that we are and become is the result of the quality of our thinking. You are today where your thoughts have brought you. You will be tomorrow where your thoughts take you.

"No matter how hard you work at becoming a top performing salesperson, if your thoughts are inundated with negativity, doubt, and fear, it will kill your efforts.

"All success comes from behavior, but all behavior starts out as a thought. I didn't get a sense that everyone understood what I said so I repeated, "All success comes from behavior, but all behavior starts out as a thought."

Karen Saltsburg raised her hand. "Help me, I'm confused. It's been over 20 years since Nike coined the phrase "Just Do It." "This launched not only one of the most successful advertising campaigns ever, but created a slogan that people use to motivate themselves to take action." Here's my question: "Can't we just 'act' our way to action?"

"Maybe you can." "However, all the reading I've done leads me to believe that every conscious act is preceded by a thought. Your dominating thoughts determine your dominating actions. The 'act' is merely the execution of thought. Thought is the power; it's the force underlying all."

"Can you imagine someone trying to 'act' their way in doing the following behaviors? If you're reluctant to make telephone prospecting calls, try 'acting' your way to make cold calls. If you're afraid of public speaking, try 'acting' your way to a public speaking career. If you suffer from Aerophobia (fear of flying) just hop on an airplane and see if that encourages you to want to fly more often. I doubt that it will."

"A friend had a tremendous fear of flying, so much that he could not fly. The anxiety was tremendous and for years he would book trips and then cancel them. He was sure he would die in a crash or attack. Attaching new thoughts to his fear of flying enabled him to take short flights. First 30 minutes, then 45 minutes, then an hour. Three years later, he is excited about airplane travel because he has attached new THOUGHTS to flying."

"Perhaps you've discover how to 'act' your way to action. If so, great! I'm convinced, however, that our brains run the show, and control what we do. You'll have a better chance of achieving long-term success if you delve into reoccurring thoughts that impede your actions. Rewire those thoughts by coming up with alternative interpretations to your original thought, and then take action.

"You'll achieve quicker results when your thoughts, feelings, and actions are all headed in the same direction.

"Successful people learn to create their own circumstances, their own experiences and results. They know what they want; they are crystal clear about their goals and objectives, and do whatever it takes to make them a reality. They are the architects of their own destiny. And, as strange as it may seem to some, the success that they enjoy, the life experiences that they live, started from a thought.

"Ideas and thoughts can hold you back, but failure is caused by inaction." I touched my temple to emphasize my point. "Thinking can be easy, action is difficult, and putting one's thoughts into action can be one of the most difficult things in the world. A thought which does not result in action is nothing but a thought.

"Until 'thinkers' get off their butts and take action, success will be just another word in the already overburdened vocabulary of the 'talkers' who just talk. Talk is cheap. It's what you do that determines your success in life. Life rewards action."

Daniels asked, "So how do I change my thinking?"

"Pay attention to it," I replied. "If you are not aware of how you interpret your thoughts and the meaning you assign to them, you have no chance to correct them." I gestured with my hands. "Changing your thoughts (especially the nagging ones) is not as difficult as it sounds. It's just a matter of having a willingness to learn to assign different meaning to them."

"Thinking is a habit, just like most other things that you do. The same way that you could improve your tennis, golf, or swimming, you can improve your thinking. However, it takes work. I probably invest twice as much time on exercising my 'mind muscles' than most people spend working out at the gym."

I extended a finger. "Pay close attention to 'trigger' events. Recognize those actions or words that derail your plans and fill your head with negative thoughts."

I extended a second finger. "If you find yourself attaching negative meaning to your thoughts and outcomes, dispute them. Ask yourself, what's the evidence that supports these conclusions?"

Now a third finger. "Find alternative ways to interpret your thoughts. With practice, you can learn to notice your own unhelpful thinking as it happens, and consciously choose to think about the situation in a more realistic and helpful way."

I walked in Daniel's direction and said, "Here's the third principle Change Your Attitude."

Key Lessons

- Selling is a game made up of an inner component and an outer component

- Salespeople who choose excellence over mediocrity think differently.

- To achieve greater success, you must first win the "inner' game" of selling.

- The key to overcoming internal barriers is self-knowledge.

- The outer conditions of your sales career will always be in sync with your inner thinking.

- It's a universal truth that your career and life moves in the direction of your predominant thoughts.

- Without the right thoughts and actions there can be no right results.

- Success comes from behavior, but all behavior starts out as a thought.

- Being a great salesperson isn't about competence, but attitude.

- No matter how hard you work at becoming a top performing salesperson, if your thoughts are inundated with negativity, doubt, and fear, it will kill your efforts.

- If you want to change your attitude the first step is to examine your thoughts.

Change Your Attitude

Daniels replied, "Change your attitude, isn't that what I've been working on all these years?"

"Have you?" I pointed out the window to the sidewalks 37 stories below. "How is it that some salespeople excel regardless of tough times? Is it family connections? Education? Experience? Financial status?"

"All of them?" He shrugged. "Guess I don't know."

"One word," I replied. "Attitude. Attitudes are the reflections of the mind. If your attitude is not programmed for success, nothing you learn, nothing you know, and nothing you do will make a difference. Being a top performing salesperson isn't about competence but attitude."

I reached into my coat and withdrew a card. "Here's another quote, this one from Charles R. Swindoll." I recited from memory. "'The longer I live, the more I realize the impact of attitude on life. Attitude to me is more important than facts. We cannot change our past. We cannot change the fact that people will act in a certain way. We cannot change the inevitable. The only thing we can do is play on the string we have, and that is our attitude."

"'I am convinced that life is 10 percent what happens to me and 90 percent how I react to it. And so, it is with you, we are in charge of our attitudes.' I gave the card to Daniels.

He read it and tucked it in his leather notebook. "That's easy to say, change your attitude and you'll change your life. But how can that happen if you don't know what to change? If changing your attitude was easy, why don't more people do it? Especially if they could be happier and more successful."

I turned from the window. "Because people make changing their attitude harder than it should be.

"If you want to change your attitude the starting point is to believe that you can change. Some people believe people can't change. When we believe we can't do something our behavior will usually confirm this."

In order to become the person you want to be, you have to believe that you can become that person. Believing you can change your attitude is the first step.

Sherman responded, "Mental conditioning?"

"Yes, a form of mental conditioning."

"Whenever you discover yourself thinking negative thoughts, instead of trying to resist the negative thought, redirect it. Think of it like mental kung fu. Take the energy of negative thinking and redirect it by assigning different meaning to it. With a little mental conditioning, whenever a negative thought occur, your mind will automatically create new meaning and put a new frame of reference around the event."

Here's an example of how it works.

If I call a client and leave three voice messages and they don't get back to me, I can tell myself this may be because:

1. Maybe they are away.
2. Perhaps they haven't picked up their messages.
3. Their voice machine isn't working and they never got my message.
4. They didn't call back because they don't want to talk to me because they don't like me.

Any of these reasons could be true, but salespeople who assign negative meaning to the event will choose number four.

"The thoughts that you most often think tend to come true. If you pour your energy into positive thinking day after day, it will become stronger and stronger."

Daniels asked, "So this mental conditioning will give me a lot more control over my thinking?"

"It becomes automatic," I answered. "At some point, your conscious mind takes over and a thought like 'I can't' automatically is REWIRED into 'How can I?'"

Daniels brightened. "I get it. When you change the meaning you assign to your thinking, you change your attitude."

Shift Thinking™ *Change Steps*

Break over, I returned to the classroom and stood before the white board. I addressed the room. "I had an interesting discussion with one of your colleagues and thought that many of you may have the same concerns. Before we move to the other principles let me elaborate a bit more on the Third Principle: Change Your Attitude.

"We've learned the importance of mental conditioning and that by assigning new meaning to your thinking, you can alter your attitude."

Jenna Gomez, a saleswoman in the front row, raised her hand. "Easy enough, but how?"

"Good question," I replied. "Use my *Shift Thinking*™ *Change Steps* to cut through the negativity in your life and open up a world of personal empowerment." *Shift Thinking* gets right to the heart of faulty thinking, helping you change irrational thinking into good thinking. Good thinking can take you to a whole new level of success - personally and professionally.

"Thoughts are neutral. Thousands upon thousands of them stream constantly through our minds, but only when we assign meaning and act on them do they have any substance."

I turned to the white board and grasped a marker. I wrote as I spoke. "Don't let the mind stand between you and your dreams."

In big red letters I wrote, "*First*, stop and think what you're thinking about." I put the marker down. "Before you can make positive changes in your attitude, you must know what's going on with your thinking and whether or not the meaning you assign to your thoughts is contributing to the situations you're struggling with.

"Ever notice how thinking occupies so much of our time? But

do you ever stop to think what you're thinking about? Have you ever thought about your thinking and how the meaning you assign to it effect everything you do and don't do?"

Jenna commented, "I think most of us go through the day on autopilot. We make hundreds of decisions every day and most of those decisions require little to no thought. We simply react to the situation."

"That's right," I replied. "We behave out of habit, necessity, or instinct. Think about it. If you've been driving for any length of time you get in the car, insert the key, and within a matter of moments you're cruising down the road. Through instinct, repetition and time, these behaviors have become hard-wired and don't require much thinking.

"However, if you want your attitude to be different, you must reclaim time to analyze what you're thinking about. Nothing will change for the better until you evaluate your thinking."

Jenna explained, "We all need quiet time to examine our lives and careers openly and honestly - spending quiet time alone gives your mind an opportunity to renew itself."

I continued with Jenna's thought, "If you are not scheduling regular time for yourself for planning and strategizing, you are creating roadblocks for future progress. I have one client, who at the beginning of the day, has started a new habit of sitting in a comfortable recliner for 10 to 15 minutes thinking strategically about his life and business. Taking that time daily helps him address his most pressing issues and open his mind to unlock new possibilities.

"For too many of us, slowing down to examine the inner-working of our mind is not appealing, and that's too bad because it's mandatory if we hope to produce the results we desire. We all need quiet time. Time to get a chance to hear ourselves think."

I wrote, "Second, identify problematic thinking - the meaning you're assigning to your thoughts that isn't helping you get closer to your goals. When you interpret a thought as negative it is important to pay attention and accept it as yours. Don't push it away or ignore it.

Train yourself, to be self-aware."

"Try these methods." I explained as I jotted on the white board, "Journaling is an effective technique to get problematic thoughts out of your mind and into the real world for analysis.

"Recording is making note of the thinking that occur to you during the day which is problematic. When you expose unhealthy thinking and record it, those thoughts immediately begin to lose power over you.

"Meditation or quiet time is another way to identify problematic thinking."

I gave the sales team a moment to catch up with their notes.

"Third, reprogram problematic thinking by using these two techniques." I held up a finger. "Learn to visualize a positive outcome for what you want to achieve. Repeat this exercise until it becomes a reality in your mind." I held up a second finger. "Get in the habit of repeating affirmations, positive statements about yourself framed in the present, as in, "'I am a great salesperson. I am successful.'"

"Every time you say something positive to yourself, you will feel better. By using positive affirmations, your life can become more enjoyable, happier and filled with more joy.

"You were born with the most powerful computer in your head. If you continually say the affirmations, eventually you'll program new belief 'files' in your mind. This process can be a little challenging in the beginning but gets easier with practice.

"Affirming what you want to believe is a powerful bridge to move you in the direction of the changes you want to make. Remember, what you believe and focus on, you will eventually create."

Phrase your desires as if they were already true, not that you would like them to be true. "'I am feeling more successful today'" is more affirmative than "'I want to be more successful.'"

"You are reprogramming your subconscious mind to believe the statements, and that helps manifest them in reality."

"And this happens...when?" An anonymous skeptical voice asked from the back.

"You must work at it," I answered, "by using the Fourth step: practice new thinking for 30 days." The most effective way to harness the power of affirmations is to repeat them to yourself on a regular basis. Repeat them mentally in the morning and evening; repeating them aloud is more effective because you can hear them more clearly. It's the repetition that adds up to the eventual grand slam.

I'm reminded of a booklet I'd read that was written in 1935 by Emmet Fox, a writer from the early part of the century. He claims you can change your life in a week if you focus intently upon your every thought. He says, "You must watch yourself for a whole week as a cat watches a mouse, and you must not under any pretense allow your mind to dwell on any thought that is not positive, constructive, optimistic, or kind."

You'll probably need more than a week to reprogram your mind. But if you follow Fox's advice, new neural pathways will eventually begin to develop in your brain.

"Now, let's go to Principle Number Four: Reprogram Negative Thinking."

Key Principle # 4

Reprogram Negative Thinking

I paced about the front of the training room. "Where do the most common, most painful, and most challenging stumbling blocks stem from?"

William Daniels spoke up, "Negative thinking?"

"That's right."

"Often, it's not our outside circumstances, our skills, our families or our businesses that keep us stuck. Instead, what tends to hold us back and hurt us the most comes from inside our minds - negative thinking."

William Daniels said, "That's my problem." I remember all the 'bad' sales calls, all my failures, and the 'good' calls and positive outcomes vanish from my mind instantly. Why does that happen?"

I walked over to William, put my hand on his shoulder and said, "Positive thinking requires effort while negative thinking comes easily and uninvited."

Daniels responded, "Okay, I understand that but where does negative thinking come from?"

"We create it from what we were told by parents, teachers, peers, and media images, and from ideas we picked up about ourselves as children. By the time average youngsters reach the age of eighteen, he or she has been exposed to negative comments and situations hundreds of thousands of times! Therefore, it should come as no surprise that most people are programmed to think negatively."

"Unfortunately, every negative thought that you replay in your mind is like an anchor holding you back. The human mind is like a sailboat on the ocean of life. As the boat sails, our thinking controls the ocean. Negative thinking creates rough seas and storms in our lives, while positive thinking creates smooth sailing."

"Are you a positive person? Are you confident and self-assured? Are your thoughts constructive and productive? When evaluating a situation do you focus on the positive side? Do you think in terms of victory and success? Do you approach life with a *can do* and *will do* attitude?"

People think they know what positive thinking is - but they often practice wishful-thinking instead. Here's the difference. Wishful thinking is saying, "I hope my sales numbers get better.' Positive thinking is saying, 'I will do whatever I have to do to make my sales numbers better."

I scanned the audience and made eye contact with as many of the salespeople as I could. "For the past 15 years, I have observed the different thinking habits and results achieved by two types of salespeople I train and coach. The *first* type of thinking is negative. This salesperson would say, 'The economy sucks, I'll never make it in sales. I can't set appointments. No one wants to meet with me. No one is buying. I don't have time to prospect for new business."

Several of the salespeople smirked in recognition of these commonly heard excuses.

I said, "The *second* type of thinking is positive. This person says, 'The economy sucks but I'll make things happen. It's not going to be easy, but I will reach my goals. There are less people buying, but people still are and I will find them. I have less time to prospect but I will make the time.'

"In both cases, each salesperson was right. Creating expectations from a negative point of view generated poor sales results. Those salespeople who approached their work with positive thinking got positive results."

Like a tally sheet, if you've got more good experiences than bad ones, the good ones dominate.

I turned back to the white board and sketched the silhouette of a head. I drew an arrow to where the brain would be. "The mind doesn't judge thoughts before accepting them. If what it hears, sees, and reads is always negative, then it accepts negative thoughts and opinions as the standard way of thinking.

"That's interesting" Sherman said. "I remember reading an article in *The Wisdom Journal* where a writer shared the following story." A Native American grandfather was talking to his grandson. He said, "I feel as if I have two wolves fighting in my heart. One wolf is the vengeful, angry, discontented one. The other wolf is the loving, compassionate, happy and contented one." The grandson asked him, "Which wolf will win the fight in your heart?" The grandfather answered: "The one I feed."

"By feeding the mind with negative thinking you personally clutter the mind and create mental speed bumps that hold you back from exploring opportunities you know are right for you, or from even recognizing opportunities that are staring you in the face."

Here are three examples of thoughts that clutter the mind:

1. Coming to a general conclusion based on a single event or one piece of data. If something bad happens once, you expect it to happen again and again. E.g., You make a telephone prospecting call and hear, "I'm not interested and they hang up."
   So you automatically think every time you make a telephone prospecting call the prospect will say, "I'm not interested and hang up."

2. Concentrating on the negatives while ignoring the positives. Ignoring important information that contradicts your (negative) view of the situation. E.g., "I know my sales manager said my presentation was good but he also said there were a number of mistakes that had to be corrected…he must think I'm really hopeless."

3. Overestimating the chances of disaster. Expecting something unbearable or intolerable to happen. E.g., "If I don't make

my sales quota for the month, I'm a failure. I'll lose my job and my life will be finished."

What you see around you, those pictures in your mind make up your life and the quality of your life. You life is merely a reflection of how you interpret your thoughts and what you believe.

I needed to make this point. To be certain I had everyone's attention, I stood on a table at the front of the training room, looked out to the audience and said, "It is impossible to perform daily activities consistently in a manner that's inconsistent with the way in which we interpret our thoughts."

If Mr. or Mrs. Negativity has climbed onboard and taken over the control of your mind, it's because you invited them in. Thoughts are visitors ...they only stay as guest if we invite them to do so.

Guarding the gate of your mind against negative thinking is your responsibility. People can affect your mind by teaching you poor thinking habits or unintentionally misinforming you, or by providing you with negative sources of influence, but no one can control your thinking unless you voluntarily surrender that control.

"If you've been thinking, 'I'm a loser,' replace it with, 'I'm a winner.' If you've been sitting around staring at your navel thinking about what you don't have, change your thinking and think about what you do have.

"To combat negative thinking, you cannot sit idly; there is work to be done. By becoming the 'observer' of your thinking and challenging it daily, you can assign new meaning to your thoughts and create a more successful life."

Jenna asked, "How do you get rid of negative thinking? Fight it off?"

"No," I replied. "Becoming aware of the meaning you attach to your thoughts puts a tremendously powerful tool in your hands. Many people, upon paying careful attention to how they interpret events, are surprised at the negativity they find there. But when we take notice of what we're thinking and what we believe in a non judgmental way, we initiate a healing process that will eventually allow us to replace unhealthy thinking with empowering thinking."

"While you can't always control conditions, you can *always* change the meaning you assign to your thoughts. You can always find thoughts that feel better when you think them. The meaning you assign to your thoughts eventually influences how you feel and act.

Jenna asked, "Can someone else make us feel a certain way? Can an event in our life directly cause us to feel happy or sad?"

Michael Edelstein, in his book THREE MINUTE THERAPY, argues the line of cognitive-behaviorists and rational emotive therapists have argued for decades. External events and people cannot make us feel any one certain way, even though it often seems that way.

"In other words, people and events do not cause our feelings - we cause them ourselves by our thoughts. This turns out to be exciting news, because that means that we have control of our feelings, much like we have control over other choices we make in our life."

Sherman followed-up with, "So, where do our beliefs come from?"

"Beliefs are formed by the stories we tell ourselves based on experiences throughout our lives. When our experiences are met with feelings, we tend to create meaning around that event, which becomes a story in our mind. Any story we tell ourselves long enough becomes a belief.

"Underlying much of our behavior is what is called a belief system. This internal system filters what we see and hear, affecting how we feel and behave in our daily lives.

"Beliefs either serve you or they don't. They either guide you toward your intended outcome or away from it.

"Choose beliefs that empower you in a way that undermines negative thinking. Once that happens, you will see positive and negative thinking for what it is--simply thinking.

"Thoughts appear and disappear rapidly, leaving no impact, until we grab-hold-of-them, shape them to our own point of view, and mold them into a belief. Once that happens, the belief remains with you until you release it."

"I've worked a lot on reprogramming unhealthy thinking and one of the most helpful things I've discovered is when a negative thought surfaces, you don't always have to come up with its opposite in order to neutralize it. If you just think about something else - and really, it can be anything else at all including stuff like what am I having for dinner, or wondering what's on TV that night - you'll displace the negative interpretation and that's often all it takes to short-circuit a chain reaction of negative thinking."

"The key is to interrupt thinking as soon as you realize you're interpreting something as being negative. For instance, if you find yourself caught in the *'I hate making cold calls'* thought pattern, you don't have to convince yourself that you *love cold calling* to break the pattern. If you can get yourself to think about anything else at all such as: *'There's nothing wrong with calling people to determine if I can HELP.'* Your focus will automatically shift and that prevents negative thinking from spiraling out of control."

I wrote a few tips on the white board and explained as I went along. "Each time you catch yourself assigning negative meaning to a thought, reject it, and think a positive one instead. *Don't visualize failure, instead visualize success.*

"*If you hear yourself utter negative words, switch to positive words.* When you say, 'I can't,' say, 'I can.'"

"Decide from today, *from this moment, you are leaving negative thinking behind and starting on a new exciting journey.*"

I walked to another section of the white board. "Now, let us proceed to Principle Five: Practice Possibility Thinking."

Key Principle # 5

Practice Possibility Thinking

"Allow me to start by quoting Darwin P. Kingsley. 'You have powers you never dreamed of. You can do things you never thought you could do. There are no limitations in what you can do except the limitations of your own mind.'"

Jenna nodded as she weighed my words.

"Think about it," I continued. "The world would stop if it were run by people who said things can't be done." I turned to my notes. "In 1899, Charles Duell, commissioner of the U.S. Patents Office, in his resignation letter, said, 'We have reached the end. Everything that can be invented has been invented.' In 1921, Hall of Fame baseball great Tris Speaker said, 'Young Mr. Ruth has made a mistake by giving up pitching to become a full-time hitter.' Later, in 1923, Robert Millikan, Nobel Peace Prize winner in physics, said, 'There is no likelihood that we will ever tap the power of the atom.'"

The audience chuckled at the absurd pronouncements.

William Daniels raised his hand. "What are you getting at?"

I answered, "Possibility Thinking." I took in his quizzical expression. "What is it? In essence, it is the management of our thinking. I took that term from Dr. Robert H. Schuller, who framed that concept by stating that we must identify impossibility thinkers. "They are the folks who judge an idea with cynicism and look for disapproval. They seek reasons why something won't work instead of visualizing ways in which it could. So they are inclined to say 'No' to an idea, never giving the idea a fair hearing."

"Self-limiting statements like 'I'm no good at this!' or 'This is impossible!' are particularly damaging, because they increase your stress in a given situation and stop you from searching for new solutions.

"The next time you find yourself thinking something that limits the possibilities of a given situation, turn it into a statement or a question. Doesn't 'I will figure this out.' or 'How is this possible?' sound more hopeful and open up your imagination to new possibilities?"

I let my comments sink in and gave the salespeople time to write notes.

I began, "Throughout my career, I've known many people who have accomplished things others were convinced they could never do. Like me, for example.

"For years, I'd thought about putting my ideas about sales in a book. Like most of you, I have a busy schedule and told myself I didn't have time to write a book. Besides, I'm not a writer. But one day I decided that I'd make the time and sat down to put my thoughts on paper. It took me four and a half years to write my first book, *The Secrets to Sales Greatness*, which I published in 2008. I kept writing and published my second book, *Opportunity Calling - The Easy Way to Double Your Number of New Qualified Appointments*, in 2010. And now *Shift Thinking*. This from a guy who had convinced himself he could never write a book!

"You must understand that what starts out as impossible becomes inevitable if you believe in your ability to push through your doubts and fears and pour all your passion into the pursuit.

"Believing in yourself and your ability is essential to make yourself a success. If you don't have this constant 'ringing' in your mind that success is possible, you won't attain it."

I projected this quote from businesswoman Mary Kay Ash on to the huge screen at the front on the training room: "Don't limit yourself. Many people limit themselves to what they think they can do. You can go as far as your mind lets you. What you believe, remember, you can achieve."

"The history of science clearly demonstrates that things are only impossible until they're not. Therefore, every salesperson should have 'impossible goals,' for it's the achievement of our impossible goals that opens new pathways to success.

"Christopher Reeve, in his book *Nothing Is Impossible*, said, 'So many of our dreams at first seem impossible, then they seem improbable, and then, when we summon the will, they soon become inevitable.'

"Consider these less than spectacular beginnings." I looked about the room and drew their attention to what I was about to write in large letters, the names Jeff Bezos and Fred Smith. "Critics and advisors told Jeff Bezos that his cutting edge startup website, Amazon.com, offered a range of products that was too broad and not economically viable.

"A Yale economics professor told young Fred Smith his term paper, based on an idea for a company that would guarantee overnight delivery to major U.S. cities, was foolish, and gave Smith a subpar grade for his work. Fred Smith went on to create the giant company FedEx."

Like every other time I mentioned these anecdotes, the salespeople laughed at how the "experts" had been so wrong.

I explained, "One thing Bezos and Smith shared was that they had the courage to challenge status quo thinking and to do the 'impossible.' Nelson Mandela summed up the reality behind many firsts when he said, 'It always seems impossible until it is done.'

To make our lives living masterpieces, we need to move beyond acceptance to the realm of possibility thinking. We live in a universe with unlimited possibilities.

The song from The California Special Olympics asks, "How far is far; how high is high?" How far is far? As far as we want to go, as far as our dreams take us. How high is high? As high as our goals, as high as the mountains we climb."

"Possibility thinking is the generation of unthought of ideas, without judgment or evaluation of any kind. While it is important to think practically, it is equally important to go beyond practical thinking. There are already enough practical voices in your head. Maybe it's time to explore thoughts that may seem shocking or crazy at first.

"By constructing more than one perspective or viewpoint, and thinking outside the box, you can make the possible far more probable."

"To get on a possibility path, you have to begin by taking your mind to a different place.

"Here are six ways to start the journey." I jotted on the white board:

1. Begin with clear thinking. Ask yourself, what do you really want in life?
2. If you know what you want ...ask yourself, why do you want it?
3. Where do you want to see changes in your life/career?
4. Stretch your possibility thinking a little every day.
5. Create a list of all the things that might make having what you want possible.
6. Dream and open your mind to imagine the best possible options and solutions coming to you.

"Take a look at your answers. When you can envision what you want, why you want it and what changes are necessary to get you there, you'll have what you need to reach your once unreachable dreams and goals. We do that by transforming the voice within."

Key Lessons

Follow these four steps to change your attitude:

1. Stop and think about what you're thinking about.

2. Identify problematic thinking patterns (thoughts that aren't helping you achieve your goals).

3. Reprogram problematic thoughts.

4. Practice "new thinking" for 30 days.

- When you change the meaning you assign to your thinking, you can change your attitude.

- There are no limitations on what you can do except the limitations of your own mind.

- Obstacles loom in front of all of us on a regular basis. But it's what you do when faced with these obstacles that will determine your level of success.

- Your 'inner voice' can be either positive or negative. It can be your best friend or your worst enemy.

- Discipline and willpower are the links between goals and accomplishments.

- It's the lack of self-confidence that sinks most sales careers.

- When you suffer from poor self-esteem, you become blind to your strong points and exaggerate your weak points.

Key Principle # 6

Transform the Voice Within

After a productive late morning session, we broke for lunch. The audience of salespeople went their separate ways while my host, Sherman Jackson, invited me to a restaurant on Fifth Avenue. We shared a small table in a corner near the back. The waitress took our drink orders.

I thanked Sherman for his hospitality and told him I enjoyed the enthusiasm of his sales team.

"Much obliged," Sherman said. "They're the best in the business. However, we all recognize there is always room for improvement. What we especially appreciate are your insights that dig deeper into the methods and techniques needed to *shift your thinking.*" He took a small note pad from his jacket and opened it to read what he'd scribbled from the morning training. "What intrigued me was your discussion on Principle Number Six: Transform the Voice Within."

The voice within--the inner dialogue. That internal voice that runs day and night prompting us - what to do, what to say, and how to feel. It's a subtle mental activity and most people don't realize it's even happening.

"Most of the time," I replied, "people just go through the day unaware of the impact their inner voices have on their everyday feelings, attitudes, and behaviors. That inner voice is a constant narrator inside your head. It has influenced you since birth and it accompanies you throughout your life from the time you wake up until you go to sleep."

"What surprised me," Sherman said, "is how much this inner voice defines and interprets our every experience."

"There is a cast of characters that live inside of us all and at different

41

times their voices can be either positive or negative," I explained. "Your inner voice can be your best friend or your worst enemy."

"The key is to turn the volume up on the internal voice of the optimist and the volume down on the pessimist. When this transformation takes place, you will create more opportunities and greater success in your life."

The waitress brought our drinks, sparkling water with lime for me, and iced tea for Sherman. We halted the conversation to peruse the menus and ordered light meals.

"What concerns me," Sherman continued as he returned to topic, "is the profound effect of negative self-talk." He circled a finger beside his temple. "That particular interior monologue is a stew of half-truths, distortions of reality, and an unbalanced focus on problems that perpetuates negative emotions. Sadly, for some salespeople, negative self-talk has become their daily inner dialogue."

"True," I said. "Inside each of us lives an inner critic with a little voice that only you can hear. This voice stirs up fear and doubt, creating internal barriers that keep you from achieving your goals. The inner critic fills your head with chatter that says:

"'I can't do it.'

"'I'm not good enough.'

"'Nobody wants to do business with me.'

"'Nothing ever goes right for me.'

"'If it wasn't for bad luck, I wouldn't have any luck at all.'"

Sherman chuckled as he wrote. "Sadly, in spite of my success, I'm too familiar with all that negative thinking."

"We all are," I replied. "What each of us wants to believe is that our inner voice has our best interests at heart. The inner voice claims to protect you from failure, embarrassment, and loss. But what you often get is an unrelenting barrage of pessimism.

"How many times have you allowed the inner critic to talk you out of something you really wanted to do or convince you it couldn't be done?"

"So the challenge is learning to distinguish between your healthy inner voice and the mumbo-jumbo of the inner critic?" Sherman asked.

"Absolutely," I answered. "We obviously have both positive and negative voices inside ourselves. The goal is to not let the voice of the inner critic to conquer your mind."

It's that inner critic who holds you back and keeps you from achieving your best. If you say, 'I deserve to be successful,' the inner critic counters with, 'You'll never amount to anything.'"

Sherman reviewed his notes and underlined a couple. "I can't tell you how many times I've allowed that inner critic to talk me out of doing something I really wanted or convinced me it couldn't be done." He flexed his big shoulders and a gloss of regret colored his eyes. "I played football in college and had the talent to play in the NFL. But I told myself it was too much of a long shot, and if I tried out, I was only setting myself up for failure and disappointment. But I saw other players who weren't any better than me make the teams and play. So I had my shot, and I didn't take it. It's a bitterness that has never stopped gnawing at me."

"That's the crux of what I'm getting at," I replied. "How many opportunities have you missed? How many hopes and dreams have you let go because the voice of the inner critic said it wasn't possible?"

"So how much control do I have over this inner voice?" he asked.

"A lot," I answered. "You can make a conscious effort to listen to your unhealthy self-talk, or you can reject it. It's a choice!"

Poet and writer, Edward Carpenter, profoundly stated near the beginning of the 20th century "If a pebble in our boot torments us, we expel it. We take off the boot and shake it out. And once the matter is fairly understood, it is just as easy to expel an intruding and obnoxious thought from your mind, as it is to shake a stone out of your shoe."

When a negative thought creep into your mind, you have the power to choose to banish the negative interpretation you've assigned to the thought and call on a more uplifting one.

"Tuning in to the voice in your head will provide you with important clues about how you view situations and why you react to them the way you do. As you become more aware of your inner voice, you realize that it has no real hold on you. You are not your inner voice, but its observer."

"How do I create a more positive narrative than the one that has been giving me so much trouble?" Sherman readied his pen over the note pad.

"Here are a few suggestions," I said. "Start paying attention to how you talk to yourself and how you present yourself to others.

"Uncover where the unhealthy self-talk originated. Earlier, I had discussed trigger events. Anticipate them and prepare yourself to address them in a positive manner.

"Recognize the down-side, meaning, what are the potholes in the road before you? Don't ignore them, but you can't let them stop your progress.

"Take proactive steps to halt the unhealthy self-talk. When that chatter of unhealthy talk starts in your head, train yourself to say "'No' to negative thinking.

"Rather than focus on problems, focus on solutions.

"Acknowledge that you are making positive changes.

"Acknowledge the things that you do well. How is it you've arrived this far in your career? It hasn't been all by accident.

"It doesn't have to be all or nothing. Look for balance.

"Allow yourself to make mistakes without self-recrimination. We learn from our mistakes. That's where experience comes from."

"And lastly, be kind to yourself."

The waitress brought our meals, a spinach chicken salad for me chicken and broccoli for sherman.

While we ate, Sherman asked about Principle Number Seven: Maximize Your Inner Forces.

Key Principle # 7

Maximize Your Inner Forces

I replied by starting with a quote of my own: "Discipline and willpower are the links between goals and accomplishment."

I explained, "Now that we've determined the need to redirect our inner voice away from criticism to positive self-talk, what's the next step? As I've mentioned before, thought without action leads to nothing. Willpower and self-discipline are two inner forces that provide the power to initiate change and achievement. In fact, willpower and self-discipline are two of the most important keys to success."

"Give me your definition of willpower," Sherman said.

"It's the inner strength to make decisions, take action and deal with any task until it is accomplished. Willpower is the ability to overcome laziness and procrastination."

"Whether we are making decisions, planning our day, or trying to directly control our behavior, we are using willpower."

He wrote in his note pad. "And self-discipline?"

"That's the ability to do what is necessary or sensible without the urging of someone else. It's the ability to get yourself to take action regardless of how you feel." I pushed my plate away and raised my hands to extend both index fingers for emphasis. "Willpower and self-discipline help us choose our behaviors and reactions, instead of being ruled by them. "How many times have you said, 'I wish I had willpower and self-discipline'? How many times have you started to do something, only to quit after a short while?" I folded my arms. "We all have had experiences like these."

"One of the most challenging problems salespeople face is the lack of discipline. They have goals they want to achieve, but lack the discipline needed to achieve them. Self discipline gives you the power to stick to your decisions and follow them through, without changing your mind, and is therefore one of the important requirements for achieving goals."

"Some salespeople seem naturally disciplined," Sherman noted, "yet self-discipline is not an innate human skill they are born with."

"True," I replied. "The selling profession is made up of salespeople who learned the art of self-discipline, and those who haven't. Some salespeople are disciplined and make things happen and others who lack discipline just hope and wish things will happen.

"Self-discipline and willpower take time to develop just like any other skill. Like the muscles in your body, the more you practice using them, the stronger they become. The less you practice using them, the weaker they become.

"The author H. Jackson Brown, Jr. once said, 'Talent without discipline is like an octopus on roller skates. There's plenty of movement, but you never know if it's going to be forward, backwards, or sideways.'"

Sherman laughed at the analogy.

I said, "The disciplined salesperson has as much control of their thoughts as a musician has control of his or her instrument. Discipline keeps the mind 'locked down' so that distraction or doubt cannot interfere with achievement."

As you know, building a business as a salesperson is a lot harder than many people expect. Anyone considering a sales career needs to ask: Can you handle 60-hour weeks? Can you handle hearing "I'm not interested" many times throughout the day? Can you handle a smaller paycheck until you build up your client base? Can you stay focused and disciplined even if your results are slow in coming?

Self-discipline means overcoming your instinctive urge to do what is easy, fun and quick. If you're having trouble making choices that allow you to sacrifice short-term pleasure for long-term success, it's time to discipline yourself to *do* what you don't want, so you can *do* what you do want.

I wrote on a sheet of paper the number 6. I said, **"Here are six things to do if you lack discipline."**

1. Schedule time for getting things done. When you schedule it, it gets done. When you don't, it won't.
2. Eliminate distractions and interruptions.
3. Follow through on what you start. If you start something, finish it.
4. Forgive yourself. You aren't perfect. No one is. Realize that beating yourself up will only make things worse.
5. Focus on motivation. What's your motivation for pursuing the goal? How will you sustain the motivation when you encounter adversity?
6. Realize that discipline is the sum of many small parts. It takes many years of small successes – and *failures*. In fact, there really is no finish line when it comes to discipline. It's a never-ending journey!

Sherman read my notes. "A journey like that will test your discipline." "You can do it," I replied. "Provided you follow my next principle: Be Mentally Tough."

Key Principle # 8

Be Mentally Tough

Sherman Jackson and I returned to his office at Palisade Global Mutual. His salespeople arrived from lunch and seated themselves back in the training room. When everyone looked ready, I began the afternoon's first session.

"So far," I said, "we've discussed the need to condition our thinking from negative thoughts and reviewed techniques to encourage positive thinking. Now let's proceed to Principle Number Eight: Be Mentally Tough.

"In all facets of life, people strive for success. What success means differs from person to person and situation to situation. It could mean making the high-school football team, having your children grow up to be respectful, or getting a promotion at work.

"The key elements of success include achieving goals, perseverance, dealing with adversity, and overcoming failure." I turned to the classroom. "What would we consider these attributes of?"

Ted Phillips, a salesman in the middle row, replied. "Mental toughness?"

"That's correct," I answered. "Mental toughness means that a person has the ability to control negative thinking so that he or she can achieve demanding goals and sustain performance under pressure."

Paul Dawson, a salesperson sitting in the second row, raised his hand. "Does mental toughness imply being insensitive and uncaring? Does it mean being bold, selfish, unethical and overly aggressive?"

"Not at all. A salesperson who's mentally tough can be quite well mannered, ethical, friendly and helpful. Quite simply, mental toughness means that an individual has the ability to master naturally unmanageable desires of the human mind."

"According to Peter Clough, a leading researcher on mental toughness, 'Mentally tough individuals tend to be sociable and outgoing; as they are able to remain calm and relaxed, they are competitive in many situations and have lower anxiety levels than others. With a sense of self-belief and an unshakable faith that they control their own destiny, these individuals can remain relatively unaffected by competition or adversity.'"

Sherman chimed in. "Would you say that mental toughness is the fortitude that allows you to overcome barriers and to step up and take a risk, even when it seems impossible?"

"That's exactly right," I said. "Mental toughness enables you to--" I wrote on the white board, "cope with the demands that are placed on you when under pressure.

"So it's a mental game?" asked William Daniels, the salesman who had spoken to me earlier.

"From my experience," I replied, "most of what occurs in sales is a mental game. Your success has to do with how hard you work and how effectively you think. However, whether you achieve your full potential is determined by how mentally tough you are.

"Just as there are those who can walk though a field of poison ivy and it never has the slightest effect on them, there are salespeople who encounter seemingly insurmountable obstacles and difficult situations and remain positive and mentally tough.

"Over the years, I read lots of books about high achievers and peak performers. Some books link success to diet and exercise. Others link success to self-promotion and marketing. Still other books link success to inter-personal skills.

"But in all of my reading and studying, I feel there is one thing that stands out above everything else in terms of what makes a salesperson successful. Any guesses?" I scanned the room.

Several salespeople replied in unison. "How mentally tough are you?"

I smiled. They were getting it. "Being mentally tough is often the last piece of the puzzle most salespeople focus on. Yet, I know few successful salespeople who are not mentally tough. If you have big dreams that you want to reach, if you want to take your sales career to that next level, then you need to learn and master these critical components of mental toughness."

I wrote on the white board and recited.

"*Self-belief.* Having an unshakable belief in your ability to achieve goals. Believe in yourself..." I wrote and underlined, *No Matter What!*

Then I wrote *Motivation* and said, "Motivation is having an insatiable desire and the self-motivation to succeed. You must be able to bounce back from mistakes and bad breaks with an increased determination to win."

Next. "*Focus.* You must remain focused on the task at hand in the face of distractions. You must learn how to switch that focus on and off. Concentrate on what is important and block distractions when necessary.

"*Stay calm under pressure.* The unexpected happens. We all face disappointments. So we must maintain our composure and know how to handle sudden negative situations.

"*Commitment.* To succeed in sales, it takes a commitment and a willingness to grow and change. Remember that the inspiration needed to become a sales champion will not come easily. It takes work."

I gave the class a moment to catch up with their notes, and then wrote on the board, Principle Number Nine: Improve Your Self-Confidence.

Key Lessons

- Most people go through the day unaware of the impact their inner voices have on their everyday feelings, attitudes, and behaviors.

- Your inner voice can either be positive or negative. It can be your best friend or your worst enemy.

- For some people, negative self-talk has become their daily inner dialogue.

- You can make a conscious effort to listen to your unhealthy self-talk, or you can reject it. It's a choice.

- Willpower and self-discipline are two inner forces that provide the power to initiate change and achievement.

- Self-discipline is not an innate human skill we are born with. Self-discipline and willpower take time to develop just like any other skill.

- Self-discipline means overcoming your instinctive urge to do what is easy, fun and quick.

- Mental toughness means that a person has the ability to control negative thoughts so that he or she can sustain performance under pressure.

- Your success has to do with how hard you work and how effectively you think. However, whether you achieve your full potential is determined by how mentally tough you are.

Key Principle # 9

Improve Your Self-Confidence

"Self-confidence is the belief that you can handle a certain situation correctly," I explained. "Self-confidence is knowing that you don't lack the skills needed to complete a task. This task could vary from being able to approach someone you don't know at a networking event, to picking up the telephone and cold calling the president of a Fortune 500 company."

David McDonald asked, "How much does your sales success depend on your self-confidence?"

Sherman and I traded knowing glances before I answered. "It's the lack of self-confidence that sinks most sales careers. If you lose confidence, you lose sales.

"Self-confidence is important in almost every aspect of our lives, especially in sales. After all, most people are reluctant to buy from a salesperson who is nervous and overly apologetic. On the other hand, buyers are persuaded by salespeople who speak clearly, who holds their heads high, answer questions assuredly, and who readily admit when they don't know something. **What expresses your level of self-confidence?**"

A saleswoman in the back answered, "Your behavior."

Someone else said, "Your body language."

Another offered, "How you speak."

"What you say."

"All true," I acknowledged. "Self-confidence is the by-product of what you believe about yourself. Self-confidence is not inherited but learned. No one lacks 'self-confidence' genes.

"Self-confidence is not a constant. People possess 'conditional' confidence. As Dallas Mavericks basketball team owner Mark Cuban used to say. "Everyone is a genius during a bull market." The condition of the market gives them the feeling that they can do no wrong. But when conditions tank, their confidence disappears.

Salespeople have different confidence levels for the activities they do. For example, you may be confident about your ability to meet people at a networking event but at the same time, you lack the confidence to make a sales presentation before a group of buyers.

"The key is to generate true confidence through living a purposeful life. All great people follow a lifestyle design that includes their values and principles. That's where the confidence comes from that allows them to face challenging circumstances head on.

"Low self-confidence is not necessarily related to a lack of ability. Instead, it is often the result of having poor self-image. Our self image develops during our childhood and is the combination of our own natural personality features together with the messages and influences we receive from those around us about how we should act and feel about ourselves.

"Many salespeople have images of themselves that are much different than their real self." I've worked with salespeople who had lots of talent, but never reached their full potential because they thought poorly of themselves.

"Whether you have sought excellence or settled for less, held back or gone after your dreams, listened to fears or charged courageously into uncharted waters, every time you face such choices you tap into your beliefs about what kind of person you are before you ever make a decision.

"Many factors affect the development of self-confidence. Parents' attitudes are crucial to children's feelings about themselves. When parents provide acceptance and praise, children receive a solid foundation for good feelings about themselves. But if the parents are too critical or demanding, or if they are overprotective and discourage independence, children may come to believe they are incapable, inadequate, or inferior.

"The good news is that building self-confidence is readily achievable, as long as you have the determination to follow things through. **Here are six steps to build self-confidence."** I wrote on the board:

1. Fill your mind with evidence of both past success and possible future success.
2. Think about your strengths.
3. Reflect on when you performed well.
4. Start to pay attention to your thoughts.
5. Commit yourself to excellence.
6. Stop looking over the fence at the Joneses.

Everybody struggles with particular things, but many of those struggles and problems are hidden from others. Instead of evaluating your strengths and your weakness based on other people, just think about yourself and how you are working on overcoming the challenges in your own life.

"Remember, salespeople who lack confidence may have the same desires as everyone else. But their goals and dreams remain unfulfilled because they don't act on them. We've discussed that before. Thought without action is nothing."

"Now that you've learned how to master your confidence, on to Principle Number Ten: Boost Your Self-Esteem."

Key Principle # 10

Boost Your Self-Esteem

"Let's back up a bit and ask ourselves, what is self-esteem? According to Nathaniel Brandend, a noted author and expert on the subject, '"Self-esteem is the experience of being competent to cope with the basic challenges of life and of being worthy of happiness.'"

"Can we define it this way?" asked Jenna Gomez. "Self-esteem is one's overall belief in their value as an individual. It implies having a sense of confidence, competence and worthiness. Healthy self-esteem lets us accept ourselves and enjoy life."

David also contributed. "No one was born with poor self-esteem. Your life experiences have taught you this self-destructive thinking. When you suffer from poor self-esteem, you feel worthless, flawed, and incompetent. You become blind to your strong points and exaggerate your weak points."

"Very good," I replied. I felt a gush of pride that happens when I click with an audience. "What I have come to learn throughout the years is that all of us have great potential. However, for many years I had trouble believing it. I grew up with low self-esteem and a lack of confidence in myself--and rightly so, as I did not know my potential and what was possible for me. I spent years looking for validation on the outside instead of realizing it was within me, just waiting to be cultivated and developed."

"Poor self-esteem and failure go hand in glove," Sherman said. "So do low self-image and poor performance. The way you feel about yourself has a huge effect on the way you treat yourself and others, and on the types of choices you make."

I added a bit more. "Salespeople with healthy self-esteem feel good about themselves and they appreciate their abilities, relationships, and accomplishments. Salespeople with poor self-esteem may feel as if no one likes them or accepts them. They don't think they are capable of doing anything well.

"Our thoughts and feelings about ourselves fluctuate based on our daily experiences. The sale you don't close, the client you lose and the rejection you experience have the potential to produce negative feelings. The occasional negative feeling may have little impact on your mood, but ongoing negativity will have a dampening effect on your self-esteem and performance.

"Research makes a direct link between low self-esteem and failure. Let's take a look at two sales reps with different perceptions of themselves. Both Debbie and Ralph have years of sales experience that includes successes and failures. One thinks highly of herself and the other one is sabotaging his career.

"When I asked Debbie to describe how she felt about herself and her sales career, she said, 'I feel great! Everything is going well. I feel like I can accomplish anything. I know everything won't be perfect, but I do know that my performance is better than average. If something goes wrong, I'm confident I can recognize what's not working and make the necessary adjustments. Life is good and I love my job.'

"When I asked Ralph the same questions, this is how he responded: 'I feel like nothing is going right. I can't close a sale or get a new appointment if my life depended on it. When I finally set an appointment, they either aren't very productive or they are cancelled. I don't think I can keep up with the demands of my sales manager. Everything seems to be going wrong. I'm beginning to wonder if sales is what I want to do. I know I'm not doing a good job. Everyone else is doing much better than I am.'"

I asked, "How many of you have heard of Joel Osteen, the popular pastor and bestselling author?"

Most in the room raised their hands.

I said, "Osteen says, 'If you see yourself as unqualified, insignificant, unattractive, inferior, or inadequate, you will probably act in accordance with your thoughts. If your self-worth is low, you will imagine yourself as a born loser, a washout, unworthy of being loved and accepted.'"

If you plant negative seeds in your brain, pretty soon your entire thought process will be negative and critical, and you become a person who sees only the negative side of everything, the proverbial 'glass is half empty' person.

I turned to the white board and wrote: *Caution.* "Self-improvement and loving yourself are not a matter of shouting to the whole world that you are perfect and you are the best. It's about acceptance and contentment. When we begin to improve ourselves, we then begin to feel content and happy. The lyrics to one of Whitney Houston's songs go, 'Learning to love yourself is the greatest love of all.' True enough. In order to love others, you must love yourself, first."

The heads nodding in comprehension prompted me to ask, "Give me the attributes of high self-esteem."

Jenna said, "Ability to accept and learn from your mistakes."

David added, "Not devastated by rejection and criticism."

William said, "Open and assertive in communicating your needs and wants."

"One more," Sherman noted, "You're able to laugh at yourself and not take yourself too seriously."

"All true," I replied. "Conversely, low self-esteem can negatively effect virtually every part of your life, including your relationships, your career, and your health.

"Now the point of this discussion is that you can raise your self-esteem to a healthy level.

Before a person can build healthy self-esteem, it helps to know what might cause those problems in the first place. Two things in particular - how others see or treat us and how we see ourselves.

Unrealistic expectations can also affect a person's self-esteem.

People have an image of who they want to be (or who they think they should be).

"If you want to improve your self-esteem, think about situations that you find troubling and deflate your self-esteem, such as making telephone prospecting calls and having potential clients hang-up on you, getting emotionally wrapped-up in a dispute with an angry customer, or asking for a referral and getting a 'no.'

"When you've identified these troubling situations, pay attention to your conditioned thoughts related to them. When I say 'conditioned thoughts' what I mean is that an event produces meaning automatically before you get a chance to think about it.

"Did you ever notice that when your thoughts turn toward the negative, your feelings about a situation affect your reaction to it? Here's an example of how easy it is to become a 'victim' of circumstances and give false meaning to events in our lives."

"I was consulting with another insurance sales team, coaching them in using the telephone to set appointments with C-level decision makers. One of the younger salesmen called a prospective client only to have him abruptly hang up. The young salesman wasn't sure what he'd done to deserve such rude treatment and that got him thinking that maybe a sales career wasn't for him. But I explained to the salesman that perhaps he had misinterpreted the prospect's behavior, and encouraged him to wait a few minutes and call the potential client back. This time, before proceeding to explain his purpose for the call, he asked the prospect if he had done anything wrong during his previous call. The prospect apologized, saying that his wife had been in a traffic accident and he was expecting a call from the hospital. That's why he had hung up so abruptly on the salesman. He thanked the salesman for being so understanding and said that if he called later, he would be willing to make an appointment. Needless to say, that prospect became a major client of that salesman. This incident turned around the salesman's thinking about making calls to prospects. He realized that by reprogramming unhealthy thinking, you simultaneously dissolve the negative feeling.

Feelings can be an important source of information. Rather than ignore or exaggerate your feelings, it is helpful to be able to accept your feelings, think about them, and learn from them. **When you are feeling a particular way consider asking yourself the following questions:**

- What is this feeling?
- What is this feeling telling me about this event?
- Why has this feeling surfaced right now?
- Is there a reason to feel differently?

"Your initial thoughts may not be the only possible way to view an event. So test the accuracy of how you're interpreting events in your life. Ask yourself whether your view is consistent with facts and logic or whether there might be other explanations for how you feel about the situation."

I readied my marker. "These strategies may help you."

I wrote and said, "Use hopeful statements. Pessimism can become a self-fulfilling prophecy. That is, if you think your presentation isn't going to go well, you may indeed stumble through it. Tell yourself things such as, 'Even though it's difficult, I can handle this situation.'

"*Take pride in your opinions and ideas.* Don't be afraid to voice them.

"*Immerse yourself.* Read books, articles, magazines that help you understand and adopt the new attitude. Watch films or listen to music that inspires you and encourages you to change.

"*Stop comparing and start winning.* There will always be some people who have more than you and some who have less. If you play the comparison game, you'll run into too many "opponents" you won't be able to compete with. If you are investing more time on watching what your competitors are doing and trying to follow their path rather than actually working on growing your business, you won't ever move forward.

"*Forgive yourself.* Everyone makes mistakes. Mistakes aren't permanent reflections on you as an individual. They are isolated moments in time. Tell yourself, 'I made a mistake, but that doesn't make me less of a person.'

"*Smile.* There's no arguing with this one -- research has shown that smiling has both psychological and physiological effects. So, put a smile on your face and you'll be on your way to feeling better.

"*Focus on the positive.* Think about the good parts of your life. Focus on what is right about you.

"*Re-label negative thinking.* Interpreting thoughts as negative doesn't mean you must choose to react negatively. Instead, think of them as signals to use new, healthy thinking. Ask yourself, 'What can I think and do to make this less stressful?'

"*Encourage yourself.* Give yourself credit for making positive changes. Tell yourself, 'I did a good job at the sales appointment. It may not have been perfect, but my colleagues said it was good.'

"To recap," I said. "This session we discussed these principles: Be mentally tough. Improve your self-confidence. Boost your self-esteem."

This segued to the second afternoon session. "We now move to Principle Eleven: Examine Your Beliefs."

Key Principle # 11

Examine Your Beliefs

A gloss of skepticism washed across the room. I sensed their concern. *What did beliefs have to do with selling?*

I waited a moment. Once I had everyone's attention I said, "You cannot succeed in sales and enjoy life with beliefs that sabotage your efforts."

I began with a question. "Where do thoughts come from?"

"The brain, obviously," someone replied.

"Close," I said. "Thoughts originate in the conscious mind and then are forwarded to the subconscious mind for processing and stored for later retrieval. These thoughts held for later retrieval are known as beliefs. They form what most of us think of as our personal reality.

"Inside our heads we have many beliefs. Some are good as they help us survive and grow. Any examples?"

Jenna Gomez said, "I believe that if I step out in front of a truck on the highway I'm going to get run over and hurt."

William Daniels added, "If I'm thirsty, I believe drinking water will quench my thirst and make me feel better."

"And there are other beliefs that are unhealthy and prevent us from being the best we can be," I said. "Beliefs are perceptions that filter communication to your brain. Beliefs are nothing more than thinking patterns that govern behavior. They can be the powerful force for creating success in your life or the shackles that stifle your potential.

"We all tend to have pre-conceived beliefs due to circumstantial influences throughout our lives, also called conditioning. By the time we reach adulthood, most people have developed their own style of responding to life's various challenges – and have also acquired quite a number of individual beliefs. Different people develop different responses, beliefs and attitudes, so that no two personalities are identical.

"We base our beliefs on how we perceive the truth, which can be false or a half-truth. Therefore, we only see what we believe or, expressed another way, we only want to see what we believe.

Irish dramatist and literary critic, George Bernard Shaw said, "The moment we want to believe something, we suddenly see all the arguments for it, and become blind to the arguments against it."

Loads of evidence suggests people tend to seek information that confirms their beliefs rather than disproves them. "Many years ago, a shoe manufacturer sent two veteran sales reps out to the Australian outback to see if they could drum up some new business. Sometime later, the company president received telegrams from both reps. The first one said, 'There's no business here...the natives don't wear shoes.' The second one said, 'There's a great opportunity here...the natives don't wear shoes.'"

The audience laughed.

"To the salesperson who sees no shoes, all the evidence points to hopelessness. To his colleague, the same conditions point to abundance and possibility. Each salesperson comes to the scene with his own perspectives, each returns with a different story."

Ted Phillips acted like he wanted to speak and he waited for the room to settle before saying, "That's a great example of how our beliefs operate. One person can view a situation as an opportunity while another equally intelligent person sees the same thing as a problem. That shows how our mind can dismiss another person's belief as being well intended but wrong, or not quite right."

"Great observation," I noted. "We begin to develop our belief systems as children. We make sense of our world by organizing our experiences into familiar belief patterns that follow us into adulthood."

I faced the white board and uncapped my marker. "Could you give me examples of personal beliefs?"

The salespeople peppered me with examples that I wrote on the board.

"I'm not good enough."

"Things will never get better for me."

"I believe in myself."

"I don't have any talent."

"I'll never amount to anything."

"I can achieve anything I put my mind to."

"Good job." I stepped back from the board to review the comments. "The 'universal law of belief' says: 'If you believe something with conviction it will become your reality.'"

"Beliefs form your inner 'rules.' Beliefs direct your behavior and determine your results."

Consider two sales managers. One sees salespeople primarily as lazy while the other sees them as desiring to do their best. Each one will look for - and see - behaviors that validate their expectations and beliefs.

"This is important," Sherman Jackson chimed in. "Your sales performance is only partially related to your potential. That is because your deep-seated beliefs create expectations about results and future outcomes. Beliefs help you discover what you want and energize you to get it."

I said, "Now understand that some people enjoy criticizing the beliefs and actions of people around them. They're quick to point out when someone else messes up. Yet when asked to examine their own beliefs and actions, they defend them as indisputable.

"It's easy to see the foolishness of other people's beliefs and actions, though it's difficult to see the error in our own ways. Other people's beliefs may seem foolish, ill-conceived or naïve, but our own are considered intelligent and well worth listening to. People believe what best fits into their own scheme of things, summarily rejecting anything to the contrary."

Jenna asked, "What happens when new information and beliefs come into conflict?"

"When that happens," I replied, "the brain does not automatically give preference to new information. This is why even irrational beliefs endure in the face of contradictory evidence."

Jenna pressed on. "So the brain doesn't care whether or not a belief matches the evidence?"

I said, "The brain cares only whether the belief is helpful for survival purposes. The brain isn't interested in reality; it's interested in survival.

"Most of us assume that if something comes to mind, it does so for a reason and must be a representative of reality. However, if you understand the principle of thought patterns, you know this is not correct. If something comes to mind, recognize it for what it is..." I wrote on the white board as I said, "a passing thought."

This was an important concept, and I gave the audience time to jot this in their notes.

I started again, "Thought as a function of thinking doesn't have any content until we attach content to our thoughts. Your beliefs, assumptions, and opinions all color the content you put into your thinking, but thought itself is an empty vacuum until you fill it with meaning.

"Think of your beliefs as a screen through which you see your world." I put my hands in front of my face and spread my fingers to look through them. "This screening process keeps you from accepting information that is inconsistent with your beliefs. Even if you have beliefs that conflict with reality, these beliefs remain true for you because they are hard wired in your mind. Your reality is the reality you decide to create."

I lowered my hands. "All of us from time to time blend our beliefs with the facts. You may think, for instance, that you are discussing the facts of a situation when you are actually talking about your beliefs. The beliefs you have about a situation are important of course, but they don't change the facts."

I reached into my jacket pocket and pulled out a Cross Pen. I held the pen for the class to see. "Suppose you perceive the color of this pen as black. Your interpretation of the color of the pen would become the belief of the color for you. If your coat looks brown to me, the fact that it is really blue doesn't change the fact that it looks brown to me. Without new input--a new way of looking at the pen and coat, or a process of defining the colors more precisely--the pen will always be black and the coat brown because we believe it is.

"Most of us live with our beliefs and haven't a clue that many are stories that aren't grounded in reality. The simple truth is that we can be horribly wrong about the beliefs that are embedded in our heads.

"Without new information, a person has only his or her own experiences and beliefs to rely on. Whatever your beliefs, you cannot change them without new meaning, a new frame of reference, new information, or a personal experience that causes you to examine and question what you believe."

William said, "I guess salespeople are no different. Like everyone else, they hold on to personal beliefs about themselves, their colleagues, the companies they work for, the products and services they sell, and the prospects they meet. However, even the most stubborn person can consider other choices, if they want to."

"That's an important point," I noted. "Increase your effectiveness as a salesperson by questioning your beliefs. Questioning your beliefs is not the beginning of a mental break-down. Rather, it is the beginning of a new life, free of the emotional baggage that has been weighing you down."

"Take time each day to ask yourself these two questions and reflect on your answers."

I wrote on the board:

What evidence are you using to support your beliefs?

"Are you analyzing all of the data that's available, or is there

information that you are intentionally ignoring?

"Beliefs are presumably quite precious," I explained. "If they weren't, each outdated belief would prove much easier to dislodge. Letting go of old beliefs is like attempting to step forward with a rubber band tied to your waist. Like the rubber band, we have a tendency to stretch only so far before snapping back to our familiar and comfortable beliefs."

Jackson nodded. He swiveled in his chair to face the audience and asked, "What would you discover if you questioned and examined your beliefs? How many outdated beliefs are you clinging to about prospecting, gatekeepers, voice mail, and closing the sale--that if examined and disputed, would prove false?"

"Good point," I said. "Disputing beliefs is the process of questioning their accuracy and possibly discovering new beliefs. The most convincing way to dispute an inaccurate belief is to show that it is factually incorrect."

"Here's an example. "There are hundreds of thousands of salespeople sitting in corporate offices clinging to the belief that telephone prospecting doesn't work. Where did that belief originate? Where's the evidence? During the past 15 years, I've developed great clients and built a successful career with my telephone prospecting efforts.

"You may prefer embracing a blind faith that doesn't require you to question your beliefs, but what happens if you're clinging to beliefs that are out-dated or wrong? Don't forget that once you accept a belief as true, your belief system makes it a fact in your mind."

I pointed to the ground. "If you saw an old sandwich lying on the sidewalk, would you pick it up and eat it?"

A grimace of disgust rippled through the audience.

"Of course not. Then why do so many salespeople pick up beliefs and assumptions and swallow them without a moment's thought? Beliefs that are out-dated and inaccurate likely contain something even more toxic than the old sandwich. The irrational beliefs you put into your head can harm you as easily as something you put in your mouth.

"Only by critical re-assessment of your long-standing beliefs can you identify their accuracy. If you temporarily suspend your conviction that all of your beliefs are true and accurate, then you may find it easier to look for evidence that both supports and weakens your beliefs.

"In your quest to reach a higher level of success, you have to examine your beliefs and determine whether they're realistic or irrational. **Ask yourself the following questions."**

I turned to the white board and asked a different salesperson to recite as I wrote.

"Is there something that I'm missing?"

"Is it possible that my thinking and beliefs could be wrong?"

"Is there a better or different approach?"

"What changes might radically improve my sales results?"

"What beliefs and thoughts have I been using?"

"What other beliefs and thoughts could I use to get a better result?"

To answer that, we advance to the next key principle: Challenge Your Fears.

Key Lessons

- It's the lack of self-confidence that sinks most sales careers. If you lose confidence, you lose sales.

- Self-confidence is not inherited but learned. No one lacks 'self-confidence' genes.

- Your initial thoughts may not be the only possible way to view a situation. So test the accuracy of how you're interpreting events in your life.

- Healthy self-esteem lets us accept ourselves and enjoy life.

- The way you feel about yourself has a huge affect on the way you treat yourself and others, and on the types of choices you make.

- Inside our head we have many beliefs. Some are good as they help us survive and grow. And there are other beliefs that are unhealthy and prevent us from being the best we can be.

- Beliefs can be a powerful force for creating success in your life or the shackles that stifle your potential.

- People believe what best fits into their own scheme of things, summarily rejecting anything to the contrary.

Key Principle # 12

Challenge Your Fears

We adjourned for the day and Sherman Jackson and I departed for dinner. Several of the salespeople, among them William Daniels and David McDonald, offered to join us for cocktails. We settled in the lounge of a local steak-house and chatted about the last topics that I'd gone over that day.

Sherman said, "I'm glad you talked about how to overcome fear and obstacles. *Fear is a big problem for most salespeople.*"

I replied, "Dale Carnegie said it best. 'You can conquer almost any fear if you will only make up your mind to do so. For remember, fear does not exist anywhere except in the mind.' Which is a great segue to Principle Twelve: Challenge Your Fears."

"That's true," Sherman offered, "the biggest obstacle that stands between you and the greatest desire of your heart is fear." He closed his eyes and recited from memory. "President Harry S. Truman had this to say, 'The worst danger we face is the danger of being paralyzed by doubts and fears. This danger is brought on by those who abandon faith and sneer at hope. It is brought on by those who spread cynicism and distrust and try to blind us to the great chance to do good for all mankind.'"

"What is fear?" Jenna asked.

"Fear is the feeling of being afraid," I answered. "Fear is an emotion that occurs in the presence of a real stimulus. It is distress aroused by danger, evil, or pain, and it doesn't matter if the threat is real or imagined."

David McDonald asked, "Is there a difference between fear and anxiety?"

"Yes." "Anxiety is a worry about something that hasn't happened yet, and the more anxious you are and the longer you're anxious, the more anxious you become. But it is not the same as fear."

Our waitress arrived and we ordered drinks, Sherman offering to buy the first round.

In our society, a lot of people believe that you shouldn't have any fear or that you should ignore it, but fear is very natural.

"We're born with fear," I said. "Psychologists tell us that every child possesses two instinctive fears from the moment of birth: the fear of falling, and the fear of sudden loud noises.

"Which means, that every other fear is created by individual experiences and natural conditioning. **What are some of these fears?**"

The replies came from around the table.

"Fear of death."

"Fear of living."

"Fear of darkness."

"Fear of failure."

"Fear of success."

"Fear of rejection."

"Fear of the unknown."

"The list is unending," Sherman noted.

"I agree," I said. "You see, fear is one of the strongest and most powerful of human emotions. It has the constrictive force of a giant python that can suffocate progress and prevent you from reaching your goals.

"Fear is a gut-wrenching combatant and top-notch motivator all rolled into one. Call it a salesperson's bogeyman."

"A motivator?" Asked David. "You mean fear can be good?"

"That's not what I said," I replied with a disarming tone. "Fear can be a great motivator to change our focus from the impossibilities of our world to the potential we have inside."

"Fears can actually lead you to greater success. Fear is a strong emotion. But that doesn't mean that it has the power to control you, or even stop you.

"Fear is a great motivator for me. I imagine delivering a keynote speech and everyone walking out saying, "What a joke." The worst thing is if people yawn and think, "Man, this is boring." Just because I'm at a certain level in my career doesn't mean fear has totally disappeared.

"I learned early in my career that if I don't have a fear that everything could go horribly wrong, it's easy for me to become complacent. Fear motivates me to work harder. Fear usually provides the initial spark that motivates me, but aspiration is also an important motivator."

While failure, ridicule or even physical danger may lie beyond the confines of comfort, reaching for new heights requires that you face your fears. Eleanor Roosevelt said, 'You gain strength, courage and confidence by every experience by which you really stop to look fear in the face.'"

"How should you react when you become afraid?" William asked. "How can you not let fear immobilize you?"

Sherman chimed in. "You have a choice. "You can continue doing what you are doing and getting what you are getting – or– you can push through your fear and begin making positive changes in your life. You don't learn, grow, or succeed if you avoid fear. You'll stay 'safe,' but you won't actually do anything, and that's far scarier."

"That's true," I rejoined. "When you avoid fear, it only grows stronger. If you attack fear with decisiveness and courage, you will find it shrivels into nothing more than a disturbing feeling."

The waitress arrived with our drinks, and we paused a moment to refresh ourselves.

Moving on, I began, "What are the symptoms of fear?" I took cocktail napkins and wrote on each, which I explained.

Indifference. "You write things off because you feel they aren't important."

Indecision. "You can't make up your mind. You think about it but don't actually do it."

Doubt. "You lack confidence in your abilities and decisions."

Worry. "You always feel anxious. You're uneasy. You second-guess yourself."

Over-cautiousness. "You're excessively cautious in making decisions."

Procrastination. "You keep putting things off until later. You defer taking action."

I passed the napkins around the table.

Williams stared at one and asked, "So the more you avoid fear, the worse it gets?"

"Absolutely," I replied. "Fear doesn't go away on its own; it gets worse and eventually snowballs out of control. If you allow it, fear will erode your self-confidence and freeze you in your tracks. The more time you spend being afraid. The more you're deprived of a fulfilling life."

"The brave salesperson is not the person without fear," Sherman elaborated, "but the individual who recognizes his or her fear and acts in spite of it" The great actor Anthony Quinn once said, 'Fear is the greatest challenge that man has. And yet, overcoming fear gives us the greatest sense of accomplishment.'"

"How do you cope?" Jenna asked. I responded, "You have a conversation with your fear and figure out how to harness it into something useful." You'll have fearful moments, but you don't have to live in fear."

I told her, "The Austrian psychiatrist, Dr. Viktor Frankl, offered a unique theory to combat fear. 'Turn fear into a ridiculous, absurd event in your mind, then allow the human reaction to absurdities to make the fear go away.' Which is what I learned to do.

"I had a ritual before making telephone prospecting calls. I would ask myself this question: On a scale of zero to death, if I make the calls, what's the worst that can happen? Knowing how ridiculous the question was, my mind would reject any thought of fear. I would chuckle for a few seconds and begin making the calls."

David added, "I remember reading what the Harvard psychologist Gordon Allport wrote, 'Any person who can figure out a way to laugh at his problems is well on his way to solving them.'"

"Good point," I said. "Fear is rooted in myth and surrounded by irrational thinking. The fears that keep you where you are do not generally reflect reality. They reflect the reality you create in your head. And a large part of that reality doesn't really exist. You are being held captive by imaginary barriers that originate in the mind."

I panned a finger across the table. "Ocean swimmers and mountain climbers will tell you it isn't the cold waters or treacherous inclines that overwhelm them, but rather the anxiety of *thinking* about the oceans and the mountains. Like the mountain climber and ocean swimmer, salespeople are also held back, not necessarily by fear itself, but more often by the thought of fear."

Fear is an unpleasant often strong emotion caused by anticipation or awareness of danger. Fear is something that everyone has to deal with.

"To become a sales champion, you must lock eyes with fear and act in ways that challenge it. Whenever a flying trapeze master takes on a new student, he asks, 'Are you afraid?' If the student replies, 'Yes, I am,' the master says, 'Good. I would be worried about you if you were not.'"

The group chuckled.

Sherman added, "At one time or another, everyone is impacted by fear. The difference between those who are successful and those who are not is that successful people keep going, despite their fear."

"How many people have the courage to face what scares them?" David asked.

"Courage is not the same as being fearless. Michael Ignatieff, a journalist and documentary filmmaker, said, 'Living fearlessly is not the same thing as never being afraid. It's good to be afraid occasionally. Fear is a great teacher. What's not good is living in fear, allowing fear to dictate your choices, allowing fear to define who you are. Living fearlessly means standing up to fear, taking its measure, and refusing to let it shape and define your life.'"

"Jenna said, "So it's not the absence of fear that makes you successful, it's the management of fear that gives you a chance to be successful." "That's it," I said.

I paused to sip my cranberry drink. "Let's return to the topic Jenna broached a moment ago. How to conquer fear?"

I raised an index finger. "First. Know the source of your fear. It's important to understand what causes you to be afraid. Here's an example. The fear of telephone prospecting usually pushes the 'fear thermometer' off the chart as soon as the idea of rejection is planted in our heads."

I raised another finger. "Second. Don't let fear impact you on a personal basis. Separate your identity (who you are) from your role (what you do)."

Finger number three. "Third. If you feel anxious or uncomfortable about a particular activity, find a way to re-frame your thinking to make it a fun and pleasant experience."

Finger four. "Fourth. When you want to overcome a fear, start small. Don't bite off more than you can chew."

Finger five: a thumb. "Fifth. Keep track of your successes. Keep a journal to record your achievements. This will help you focus on what's working."

The index finger of my other hand. "Sixth. Use your right brain more often and unlock your creativity."

And one more finger. "Seventh. Things get easier the more you do it. So keep doing it." I let my comments simmer before continuing

"Now we're at Principle Thirteen: Beat Rejection."

Key Principle # 13

Beat Rejection

"Mankind has overcome hardships and natural disasters. Yet there is one fear that defeats salespeople more than any other fear--the fear of rejection. While rejection is but a word, its destructive force is as strong as a bull."

David asked, "How can one tiny word, *No*, evoke so much fear in the hearts and minds of so many salespeople?"

I answered, "Research suggests there is a genetic predisposition to be innately sensitive to rejection. Somewhere within most of us, rejection triggers a degree of fear."

"This is an important point," Sherman said. "Fear of rejection is the irrational fear that others will not accept you for who you are, what you believe, and how you act. It's a state of mind that makes you incapable of doing or saying anything for fear of others' lack of acceptance. This attitude encourages ongoing irrational thinking and behavior, resulting in personal stagnation."

I looked around the table. "When you approach a prospect either by phone or in person, you face the risk that someone might reject you. But when you avoid prospecting because you fear someone might say no, you miss out on the opportunity where a prospect or customer will say 'yes.'

"One major difference between average salespeople and top performers is how they handle rejection. If a prospect says 'no,' sales champions don't take the rejection personally. They move on and look for the next prospect."

Each of us has an identity and various roles. Our identity consists of our values, self-concept and self-worth. The roles we carry in life vary. There are our roles as a husband/wife, father/mother, salesperson, banker, fireman, nurse, golfer, etc. Being able to separate your role from your identity and not let rejection negatively impact who you are is your edge to succeed.

The success or failure of your various roles in no way measures your worth as a human being. When you confuse who you are with what you do, you jeopardize your ability to bounce back, learn important lessons and move on with your life.

William offered, "I once received this fatherly advice from a friend. 'Your degree of success is in proportion to how many no's you can sustain while pursuing your goals and dreams. The number of no's you are willing to move beyond to get to your desired goal will dictate whether you succeed or fail.'"

I directed everyone to turn to page 18 in their handouts. "How many of you are familiar with Jack Canfield and Mark Victor Hansen?" Most of the audience raised their hands.

Mike Kelly, a veteran member of the sales team said, "Jack Canfield and Mark Victor Hansen are coauthors of the world renowned *Chicken Soup for the Soul* book series. I've enjoyed reading their books." "You're right; I've enjoyed their books as well." I explained that the tale of the *Chicken Soup for the Soul* series is a great testament to what it means to beat rejection. "I love the story of how it came into existence. The authors were turned down by 33 of New York's biggest publishing houses in the first month of their efforts to promote their labor of love! They heard, 'We don't think there is a market for this book.' 'We just don't get it.' 'The book is too positive.' 'It's not topical enough.' All totaled, they were rejected by 130 publishers. To top it off, their agent said, 'I can't sell this book - I'm giving it back to you guys.' They finally found someone willing to take a risk on their project. The first books were published on June 28, 1993, with over 112 million copies sold to date, about 200 spin-offs in print and translations in over 40 languages."

Jack Canfield and Mark Victor Hansen were able to accomplish their goals and beat rejection because they believed in their work and refused to quit.

"When you get rejected, how do you feel?" Jenna tossed the question at me. "Do you feel like you lost your best friend, instead of just losing a sale?"

"It shouldn't," I replied. "It is inevitable you will be turned down at various points in your life and career. However, if you take rejection personally it will negatively affect your mood, behavior and your sales results."

Mike Kelly asked, "Is rejection the real problem in sales?"

"Rejection is not the problem," Sherman explained. "The problem is how salespeople condition themselves to think about rejection. For example, most people are conditioned to feel some level of anxiety if they are criticized, if they don't live up to expectations, or if they are rejected."

"I agree," I answered. "Your reactions to rejection depend on the meaning you assign to your thinking which impact your feelings. Let's suppose your boss calls you into his office and fires you from your job. Later, you tell a friend that your boss ruined your life. You may believe the firing caused you to feel a certain way.

"But don't get caught in the trap of irrational thinking. Don't accept the false premise that your feelings and behaviors are controlled by the events in your life. Situations in and of themselves do not produce feelings. It is your perception of the situation that makes you feel happy or sad.

"How you interpret challenges, setbacks, and criticism is your choice. You can interpret them as problems or you can interpret them as signs that you need to reevaluate your strategies, stretch yourself, and expand your abilities. It's up to you.

"What you see, hear, feel and learn is processed through your mind. If two salespeople attend a networking event, visit with a potential client or close a sale, they will each report a different set of experiences because of how they processed the circumstances through their own thinking."

I grabbed another napkin and wrote a big number 10. "I believe that 10 percent of your attitude is determined by what life hands you and 90 percent by how you choose to respond. Remember, it is not so much what happens to you that actually makes a difference; it is rather what you do with what happens to you that determines your outcome.

"You are empowered to create your own reality. You are the only one who can put meaning in your head. You are in charge of how you interpret your thoughts; you decide which ones to cultivate and bring into reality and which ones to cast aside."

"I understand," William said. "Rather than cling to some irrational thought like, 'rejection means I'm a failure,' we should incorporate new positive meaning about how we look at and respond to rejection. When negative thoughts come up, this is the time to take mental control. Give these thoughts no importance and let them go."

"Precisely," I replied. "Meaningless events cannot cause feelings of rejection. Rejection comes from the interpretation you give events in your life.

For example, imagine the following situation. A friend is due to meet you at your house for dinner at 6:30 p.m. But it's now past 8:00 p.m. and there is no sign of her - not even a phone call. What meaning would you assign this situation? There is more than one possible answer. You might interpret the event:

1. She might have been hurt or injured on her way to your house.
2. How rude. She didn't even bother to let me know she was going to be late.
3. She's late because she didn't really want to have dinner with me because she thinks I'm boring.
4. She's probably just delayed. That's okay because I can use the extra time to clean-up the house and get dinner ready.

Of course there are many other interpretations for a friend being late for dinner. Therefore, there are many possible reaction to the same event.

"To beat rejection don't jump to the worst conclusions without thinking of any other possibilities. By assigning new meaning to your thinking you can cut the 'belief chain' of the past so you can live a more promising life in the future."

"Two salespeople I coached named Michael and Ed work for the same company and have been in sales there for the same number of years. In the past 12 months, Ed's gross sales commissions amounted to $62,000 and Michael's were $164,000. Although I was able to pinpoint some minor contrast in their skills, the difference maker between Michael and Ed is how they process the thought of rejection in their heads.

"When Ed thinks about prospecting, he worries about being rejected. Unlike Ed, Michael is eager to prospect and isn't worried about the possibility of being rejected. He has no problem picking up the telephone and calling strangers, asking for referrals, and knocking on doors because he knows he will eventually find someone he can help."

David said, "Then the message is, how you handle rejection depends on how you choose to interpret the messages conveyed to you and how you choose to process those messages."

"That's right!" I exclaimed. "Your response to rejection and the influence it does or does not have on you is a choice." I raised my cocktail glass to salute him. "Your choice!"

But that was not the end of the lesson. It would continue when I told them about Principle Fourteen: Confront the F-Word.

Key Principle # 14

Confront the F-Word

After Happy Hour, the other salespeople left the steak house. Sherman Jackson and I took our drinks from the bar to the dining room. A guest joined us at our table. He was slightly built, younger man with an easy-going manner which contrasted with his intense eyes. His name was Parnell Smith and he was a longtime business acquaintance of Sherman.

The waitress brought our menus.

Parnell said, "Sherman says you're in town teaching a sales seminar."

I acknowledged that I was. Sherman explained how he had heard me speak in Las Vegas and then offered to bring my "*Shift Thinking*" message to his sales team.

We ordered dinner. I asked for filet mignon; Parnell, skirt steak with artichoke; Sherman, beef medallions with red wine sauce and mushrooms. Parnell asked what topics I'd addressed so far. I told him that our final session of the day covered Principle Fourteen: Confront the F-Word.

He cleared his throat. "The F-Word? Let me guess...Failure."

"It's what some people fear most and why I encourage my clients to confront the dreaded F-Word."

"It's practically a taboo subject," he offered. "How do you even begin to address it?"

"I explain to people, 'Every problem or obstacle you face has been presented to you for the purpose of teaching life's lessons that allow you greater clarity.'

"People dislike failure because failure doesn't look good on résumés, financial sheets, and scoreboards. Society doesn't reward failure, and you won't find many failures documented in the history books."

"There are exceptions," Sherman chimed in. "The exceptions are those failures that became springboards to later success."

"Failure seems to be a prerequisite to success," I declared. "There is no success story that does not include a chapter or two in which failure seemed imminent, with the desire to throw-in-the-towel in plain view."

The achievers of this world are not discouraged by initial failure; this is fundamental to their success. Look at Thomas Edison. When he sought to invent the light bulb, it purportedly took him 1,000 tries before he developed a successful prototype. When asked, "How did it feel to fail 1,000 times?" Edison responded, "I didn't fail 1,000 times. The light bulb was an invention with 1,000 steps."

"Extraordinary leaders believe the most regrettable failure in life is failing to fail," says Gary Burnison, author of *No Fear of Failure.* "It is only when we make mistakes in performance that we can really begin to notice what needs attention."

Parnell Smith added, "The only time we ever know what's really going on is when the rug's been pulled out and we can't find anywhere to land. We use these situations either to wake ourselves up or to put ourselves to sleep."

I said, "We are programmed at an early age to think that failure is bad. This belief is misguided and prevents people from learning from their missteps. But in sales, failure is sometimes bad, sometimes inevitable, and sometimes even good."

"Good?" asked Parnell. "How so?"

"Because," I answered, "learning to fail and learning from failure are key ingredients to success."

Sherman articulated, "Sales champions know the difference between failure and temporary defeat. They aren't afraid of failure and they understand that knowledge comes from making mistakes."

Our meals arrived. As we ate, I explained, "Even for top performing salespeople, long track records of success are punctuated by slips, slides, and falls. Great salespeople face the same challenges as average salespeople, but they respond differently, as I found in the research for my book *The Secret to Sales Greatness*. Great salespeople look at failure and channel it into something positive. They remain calm, learn, adapt, and persevere when dealing with failure. Like great trees, great salespeople grow stronger when exposed to powerful storms."

"Cavett Robert, founder of the National Speakers Association, wrote, 'If we study the lives of great men and women carefully and unemotionally, we find that, invariably, greatness was developed, tested, and revealed through the darker periods of their lives. One of the largest tributaries of the River of Greatness is always the Stream of Adversity.'"

"That reminds me of Michael Jordan, the legendary Chicago Bulls basketball star," Sherman rejoined, "who was quoted on a poster as saying, 'I've missed more than 9,000 shots in my career. I've lost almost 300 games. Twenty-six times, I've been trusted to make the game-winning shot and missed. I've failed over and over and over again in my life. So that is why I succeed.'"

"A great example," I concurred. "Remember, the only salespeople who never fail are those who refuse to take the first step. Confucius taught, 'He who tries something and fails is infinitely greater than he who tries nothing and succeeds.' Doing something new is inspiring even if you don't succeed.

"One mantra of modern business is that nothing is a better teacher than failure. The prevailing school of thought at some successful companies--such as General Electric, Corning and Virgin Atlantic--is that great success depends on great risk, and failure is simply a common by product.

"At Sure Payroll, a $23 million dollar online payroll-processing company based in Glenview, Illinois, they actually have a reward for the 'Best New Mistake.' Here's what their president, Michael Alter, had to say about failure, "'In a culture of innovation, failure is always an option. If you don't encourage people to take risks, then you end up with incrementalism forever. Mistakes are the tuition you pay for success.'"

Sherman spoke up, "Bad habits die hard, especially in an organizational climate that provides no incentive to take risks."

"Don't get me wrong," I said. "Good salespeople are careful not to make mistakes. Sales champions often make mistakes because they are not afraid to take thoughtful risks and fail. For successful salespeople, it's virtually a badge of honor to have stumbled, even spectacularly, on their road to success.

"With every failure comes the chance to learn something new. Failure is a steppingstone to greater success. Author Roger Von Oech said this about failure: 'Remember the two benefits of failure. One. If you do fail, you learn what doesn't work. Two. Failure gives you the opportunity to try a new approach.'"

"I get it," Parnell replied. "To deal with temporary setbacks, seek the lessons they hold. If you prematurely judge something as a failure when you're still in the learning process, you will prevent ongoing development."

"Absolutely," I replied. "John Amatt, founder and president of One Step Beyond, once said, "The only failure in life is when we fail to learn the lessons from our experiences."

"When failure happens, reassure yourself that you can learn a great deal from your failures if you resist the temptation to ignore them, or condemn yourself for having failed in the first place. **Here are the steps to overcome the fear of failure."**

Since I like visual aids, I wrote notes on pieces of notebook paper:

1. Take action. Bold, decisive action! Do something that scares you, such as making a cold call to the president of a large company. It's important to overcome the inertia by doing something bold.
2. Be persistent. Successful salespeople don't just give up. Every day they get out of bed, put one foot in front of the other, and

keep going. Try different approaches to achieve your outcome until you finally get the results you're looking for.

3. View it differently. View failure as temporary.

4. Do things differently. If what you are doing isn't working, do something else. There is an old saying, "If you always do what you've always done, you'll always get what you always got." If you're not getting the results you want, then you must do something different.

5. Don't take failure personally. Failure is not a personality flaw. Keep your identity separate from your sales role. Failing to achieve a specific sales outcome shouldn't negatively affect you as a human being. Separate who you are from what you do.

6. Don't be so hard on yourself. Leave that job to your prospects. They'll find plenty of reasons to make your job difficult.

William Daniels said, "There is no failure, only feedback. So I keep asking, what's the feedback telling me?"

"If you want to succeed, you must learn how to fail successfully. Sounds counter-intuitive huh? But it is one of the most important business concepts I've learned. If you don't fail and learn, you are not stretching out of your comfort zone. You are not taking risks. You are not learning."

We finished dinner. The waitress cleared our plates and brought coffee and dessert.

I continued, "Once you've confronted the F-Word, it's time to advance to the topic I'll cover in tomorrow's lesson; Principle Fifteen: Have Courage to Change."

Key Lessons

- Fear is one of the strongest and most powerful of human emotions. It has the constrictive force of a giant python that can suffocate progress and prevent you from reaching your goals.

- You don't learn, grow or succeed if you avoid fear. You'll stay safe, but you won't actually do anything, and that's far scarier.

- If you attack fear with decisiveness and courage, you will find it shrivels into nothing more than a disturbing feeling.

- One major difference between average salespeople and top performers is how they handle rejection. If a prospect says "no," sales champions don't take the rejection personally. They move on and look for the next opportunity.

- The success or failure of your various roles in no way measures your worth as a human being. When you confuse who you are with what you do, you jeopardize your ability to bounce back, learn important lessons and move on with your life.

- Failure seems to be a prerequisite to success. There is no success story that does not include a chapter or two in which failure seemed imminent with the desire to give up in plain view.

- Learning to fail and learning from failure are two key ingredients for success.

Key Principle # 15

Have Courage to Change

The next morning, Sherman Jackson and his salespeople had their coffee handy and looked eager.

I opened with the morning's topic: "There are only a few certainties in life: death and taxes…and change.

"Everything changes. Lao Tzu, writing in the Tao Te Ching said, 'The only thing that is permanent is change.'"

"I need to emphasize," Sherman added, "that today, the speed of change demands a completely different sales professional. One who understands that the traditional 'yellow-brick-road' to success has been turned-up-side-down."

He elaborated, "There was a time when a salesperson did not really need to be very proficient at prospecting and selling. I'm not suggesting that the sales profession was ever easy. However, to succeed in the past, all you needed was a pleasant disposition, reasonable social skills, and the ability to position yourself as the client's friend.

"Occasionally, you'd do a favor for a client. You'd call on him to convey your regards and pass him little gifts like tickets to local sporting events or maybe a round of golf.

"You'd sit in his office, have a cup of coffee, and listen to him mouth off about how he was the only one in his company who knew what he was doing. Then, once in a while, he'd hand you a purchase order for your product or service and you would return to the home office, triumphant and secure in the knowledge that you were at the top of your profession."

"Times have changed," I emphasized, "Buyers have become more sophisticated, and they have more options. Technology has wired us all directly to each other. Now every company and salesperson has instant access to everyone, everywhere."

William Daniels said, "Accepting that the sales profession is evolving and requires change is not an indictment on past thinking. Smart salespeople make decisions based on the current facts and situations at hand. When those facts and situations change, it's naïve to think that the way we've always done things will be a winning strategy for the future."

Ted Phillips spoke up. "To change the current selling paradigm, we must open ourselves to ideas and thinking that initially may seem counterintutive to the way things have always been done. One way is to jettison some of our most cherished core principles of selling - principles that used to work, but no longer do."

I agreed, "We desperately need new thinking to transform how we do business. The salespeople who are winning in the new century leapfrog their competitors by thinking differently. Without knowing the buyer's hidden thoughts and feelings and the forces behind them, it will be difficult to solve their real problems."

Just like driving a car, you never hold the wheel in one position all the time. If you did, you'd eventually run off the road. Instead, you constantly make little adjustments to remain on the road. The same principle applies to sales.

We're living in a different era, a different age. An age in which those who 'think and sell differently' will be valued even more than ever. To exploit new opportunities, salespeople must know significantly more than they currently do about how customer's think and act.

Every salesperson today competes based on his or her value proposition and how they're able to differentiate themselves from their competition.

The real value is what salespeople bring to their prospects and clients with their questions, compelling visions, and their ability to integrate ideas and solutions into competitive advantages.

Salespeople must pinpoint where prospects and customers are losing revenue and failing to take advantage of opportunities. They must diagnose the prospect's current situation. Help customers unearth and comprehend their most compelling problems. Help them recognize the emotional pain they're experiencing in the absence of their solution, anticipate and respond to problems they will face in the future, and help them manage the pain of change they will no doubt go through as they implement new solutions. In short, you must help your clients provide greater value to their customers and become an indispensable trusted advisor.

"This *'shift-thinking'* selling approach requires adopting the mind-set of a physician."

Parnell lowered his cup of coffee. "A physician? Like a doctor?"

"Yes," I answered. "Because like a doctor, it's the salesperson's responsibility to examine the health of his prospects' and clients' business situations and make educated recommendations that lead to healthier profit margins."

Sherman confided, "It's become a deeper, more complex process than most salespeople are accustomed to. But, if you want to maintain a competitive edge in a time when your prospects and customers have an endless supply of choices, you have no alternative but to reinvent yourself."

I addressed the room. "Ask yourself these questions: Are you still trying to win clients with the lowest price, by being the person who does a few little favors in a win-lose relationship? Or are you a professional salesperson, in an equal partnership with prospects and clients who respect and trust you?"

I said, "This is the perfect time to re-evaluate what has worked well and what has not, and what you need to do differently to meet the challenges in front of you. That's what it means to have courage to change."

Key Principle # 16

Accept Responsibility

"We left off by acknowledging we must possess the courage for change," I said. "We do that by addressing Principle Sixteen: Accept Responsibility." I looked at the audience. I said the prompt, "And what is responsibility?" as I wrote on the white board: *Responsibility is the price of greatness. – Winston Churchill*

Turning back to the room, I asked, "Who decides if you will be successful?"

Hands were raised, and a collective, "Me," echoed.

I panned the marker across the room. "That's correct. Each of you is responsible for your success. And if you want more success, you have to accept 100 percent of the responsibility for whatever happens in your life."

One of the most important personal decisions you can make on your road to becoming a sales champion is to tear down the mask of defense or rationale for why others are responsible for who you are, what has happened to you and what you are bound to become. We can and must accept responsibility for our lives.

This acknowledgement has been the defining moment for many great achievers throughout history.

I wrote on the board: *Excuses*, and X'd it out.

"Sales champions take responsibility for their results. They don't blame internal problems, the economy, the stock market, tough competitors, or anything else if they fail to meet their goals. They know that their thinking and actions will determine their results and they practice 'good' thinking and do what is necessary to succeed.

Salespeople must stop making excuses for not:

- Setting more qualified appointments
- Getting more referrals
- Closing more profitable sales

None of these excuses will ever turn into a success story.

"You will never accomplish anything of value, without first accepting responsibility for your life. Whether you are an average or extraordinary salesperson, you must take credit or blame for where you are today. Everything you are and everything you become is up to you."

Sherman added, "Taking responsibility can be scary. A client told me, 'It's like taking a parachute jump. It's frightening and exhilarating at the same time.' No one wants to be held accountable if things don't work out but in reality, the act of not accepting responsibility will leave you much worse off than the alternative."

"Very true," I replied. "Personal responsibility includes..." I recited as I wrote on the board, "Acknowledging that you choose the direction of your life and career.

"The belief that you are responsible for determining who you are and how your choices affect your life.

"Recognizing that it's not healthy for you to depend on others to make you feel good about yourself.

"Accepting that you are solely responsible for what you choose to think, feel and do.

"Accepting responsibility means that you refuse to criticize or blame others for any reason.

"Developing positive self-talk to enhance your personal development."

I stepped from the board and faced the room. "Self-responsibility is accepting yourself as you are. Blaming others for your deficiencies won't help you become a better salesperson. It's easy to blame someone or something other than yourself but if you are looking for more success, you need to accept and take responsibility for who you are and what you do."

I returned to the board. **"To determine if you're having problems accepting personal responsibility, answer the following questions."**

Again, I read aloud as I wrote:

"1. How easy is it to accept that you are responsible for your choices?

"2. How easy is it to blame others for where you are today?

"3. How often do you feel sorry for yourself?

"4. How easy is it to accept blame or admit mistakes?

"5. How easy is it to accept that you and you alone, determine your feelings when events occur in your life?'"

The salespeople busied themselves taking notes.

When they were done, I commented, "Easier said than done, for sure."

David McDonald waved his hand. "Then how do you avoid the excuses trap?"

"By advancing to Principle Seventeen: End the Blame Game."

Key Principle # 17

End the Blame Game

I paced between the white board and my audience. "In our culture, there's the tendency to blame others for our problems. Society is plagued with the 'it's not my fault' mentality. The reality is: it probably is your fault.

"The hallmark of mediocre salespeople is to blame others for the things that go wrong in their lives. And yet, finger pointing is one of the surest ways to remain in a losing situation.

Webster defines blame as: "To find fault with, to hold responsible."

"When you blame someone else, you are not taking responsibility for yourself or your circumstances. As a result, you think of yourself as a helpless victim and if you function in a helpless way, you'll convince yourself and others that you are indeed incapable.

"You have no excuse to be a victim and blame others for your shortcomings. Your boss is not responsible for your low salary. Your sales manager is not responsible for your poor closing ratio. Your parents are not to blame for your lack of success and your friends are not to blame for your lack of happiness in your life.

"What we don't realize is that we can build a life full of joy for ourselves so that each day can be brimming with fullness. To do that, we need to create it for ourselves by accepting responsibility."

I sketched a picture of an ostrich on the board. "The ostrich has a peculiar habit. It likes to hide its head in the sand. If you choose to believe you are a helpless victim of circumstances beyond your control, you're like the ostrich and there's not much I can do for you. Hiding your head in the sand and making excuses might be a temporary coping mechanism, but the long-term result is often more failure.

"The next time you blame someone for your struggles, consider the proof that supports your contention that others are at fault. Take an honest inventory of your strengths, abilities, talents, and positive points, and then accept responsibility for who you are.

"How many of your problems would disappear if you accepted personal responsibility? What goals and dreams would be realized if you were to tear away the rationale for why others are responsible for who you are, what has happened to you, and what you are to become?"

I instructed the salespeople to turn to page 27 in their sales handout. "George Bernard Shaw, the world-renowned Irish author, said..." I read from the handout, "'People are always blaming their circumstances for what they are. I don't believe in circumstances. The people who get on in this world are the people who get up and look for the circumstances they want, and if they can't find them, make them.'"

I put my handout down and turned again to the white board. "Blame is."

I wrote and said, "A crutch.

"A distraction from what's real.

"A reason to not give it your best shot.

"A barrier to the future that forces us to live in the past."

"I meet a lot of people (and I've been guilty of it myself) who will deflect blame onto someone else, even when there really isn't any blame to be had. It may make you feel better, but it's not going to make anything actually *be* better."

"You are responsible for your happiness, for your fitness and health, for your relationships, for your finances and for all your actions. Have you been hiding from that responsibility? Have you been blaming your unhappiness and incompetence on others? If so, it's time to stop blaming others and taking responsibility for your own life. That's when you really start to live."

I read from page 28 of the handout. "Dr. Wayne Dyer, a popular self-help advocate, author, and lecturer, said, 'All blame is a waste of time. No matter how much fault you find with another, and regardless of how much you blame him, it will not change you.'"

Powerful words. I let them simmer with the audience.

"Here's another quote: "Benjamin Franklin said, 'He that is good for making excuses is seldom good for anything else.'

"Which is a great segue to Principle Eighteen: Stop Making Excuses."

Key Lessons

- Today the speed of change demands a completely different sales professional. One who understands how to think outside the box.

- The salespeople that are winning in the new century leapfrog their competitors by thinking differently, making adjustments and playing by a different set of rules.

- Every salesperson today competes on his or her value proposition and how they're able to differentiate themselves from the competition.

- If you want more success, you have to accept 100 percent of the responsibility for whatever happens in your life. Everything you are and everything you become is up to you.

- Sales champions take responsibility for their results. They do not blame internal problems, the economy, tough competitors, or anything else if they fail to meet their sales quotas.

- All blame is a waste of time. No matter how much fault you find with another, and regardless of how much you blame them, it will not change you.

- The next time you blame someone for your struggles, consider the proof that supports your contention that others are at fault.

Key Principle # 18

Stop Making Excuses

Sherman stood and announced, "The truth is that every human since the beginning of time has made excuses, and everyone will keep making excuses. Our aim is not to eliminate every excuse uttered by every person on Earth. Rather, it is to help you eliminate the excuses that prevent you from reaching your full potential."

I thanked Sherman for his timely contribution and continued, "There are two types of salespeople: those who make excuses and those who get things done. An excuse salesperson will find any excuse for why a job was not done, while a results salesperson will find a reason why it can be done.

"Excuse-making is one of the most destructive barriers to self-improvement and self-realization. I've learned that successful people drop the excuses and take full responsibility for their lives. As a result, they don't just get what they want in life—they get the life they always wanted.

"Excuses are contagious and self-defeating. Rather than take a setback in stride, unsuccessful people hunt for scapegoats, laying blame on everyone but themselves. ."

"I learned long ago that it is easier to turn a failure into a success than it is to turn an excuse into an opportunity. A salesperson can fail, then learn from his or her failure, and convert that experience into an opportunity. A salesperson who makes excuses and refuses to accept responsibility has little chance for improvement."

"It is painful to admit your faults and confront your excuses, but the pain you experience during the initial examination phase is the first sign that the transformation from weakness to strength has begun.

"The truth is that the more you make excuses, the more excuse-making becomes a part of you. If you focus on results, you achieve them; if you focus on having excuses for failures, that is precisely what you will find."

I read the skepticism in their faces. "Let me repeat. The more you make excuses, the more excuse-making becomes a part of you.

"What are three steps for dealing with excuse-making and making sure that it becomes a thing of the past?"

David answered, "Catch yourself making the excuse when it happens."

Jenna Gomez added, "Reframe the excuse and either state clearly or write down why it is not true."

I said, "Give us some examples."

She proceeded to the white board at the front of the room and began writing.

I explained her notes. "Here's the excuse: Our price is too high – Here's the reframe: Sell value not price; amateurs sell price.

"Here's the excuse: I have no time for prospecting – Here's the reframe: Create time, plan ahead, stick to a schedule, and eliminate time wasters.

"Here's the excuse: My goals are too high – Here's the reframe: Stay committed and plan steps to achieve your goals.

"Here's the excuse: No one is buying now – Here's the reframe: Create urgency and value; most companies have budgets and will make decisions if shown value.

"Here's the excuse: I can't get prospects to return my calls – Here's the reframe: I will give prospects reasons to call me back.

"Here's the excuse: All I need is more leads – Here's the reframe: Identify your best leads and get to them by yourself, you cannot wait for them to find you."

William Daniels offered this suggestion, "Prescribe a course of action that will eliminate the excuse for good and set you on your way to success."

"All correct." "I smiled in appreciation. Sherman had a bright sales force.

What are your excuses?

It's important to acknowledge those excuses that have held you back in the past. Get a piece of paper and write down any reasons which you use to convince yourself that you don't want to change, or which make you feel you can't change.

How to stop making excuses and start building a successful sales career:

1. Realize that your success or failure depend on you. It depends on the choices you make. It depends on your attitude.

2. When you make a mistake, accept responsibility; learn from it; and don't repeat it. Use your time for discovering solutions instead of inventing excuses.

3. List all your excuses for why you have not, or cannot accomplish a specific goal. Now, go through each one and find ways to get around, or solve, each one. There is always a way!

4. From time to time, stop and examine your progress. Compare where you are now with where you would like to be. Ask yourself why is there a gap between these two points. Don't make excuses. Take corrective action.

"Now, on to Principle Nineteen: Quit Lying to Yourself."

Quit Lying to Yourself

"It's one thing to be deceived by another person, and something quite different to fool yourself by engaging in self-deception and outright lies. Whereas lying to others is selfish, lying to ourselves is plain stupid.

"We may not initially recognize how much we do lie to ourselves. It is an easy thing to deny because there is no solid evidence that we do so. We do not utter the lie aloud, and no-one is there to hold us accountable. Thus, it is easy to pretend that it never happened, thereby lying to ourselves yet again.

"The reason that we lie is to stop ourselves from being hurt, usually to protect our self-worth. There are thoughts that we find unacceptable, and thus we simply refuse to acknowledge them. We hope that soon the reality will change and that the lie will be inconsequential. For example, we may deny that we are reluctant to make telephone prospecting calls, hoping that soon the reluctant behavior will go away. Our reasoning is that if it does go away then our lies will no longer matter, and we will have avoided dealing with a painful reality.

"Human beings are pros at lying to themselves. Many people navigate through life with blinders over their eyes because they feel it's easier to avoid the truth than to face it.

"People actively deny the truth about themselves until they are forced to deal with it. For better or worse, we convince ourselves of things that are not true about the most basic things in life: Who we are and what we're doing."

Jenna Gomez asked, "How can I know myself?"

I answered, "By making yourself fully aware of what makes you tick." How many times this week have you sat down and thought about yourself? Nothing specific, just a general observation of who you are and what you're doing?"

I got my marker ready to write. The quest to discovering your authentic self starts by:

1. Observing who you are.

2. Knowing who you are.

Living authentically is never easy. It can be hard work, but the rewards are certainly worth the effort. The work begins with asking two questions.

Do you know the real you? Or are you living a compromised existence? When you lie about who you are and what you believe, you're bound to live a life filled with inner-conflict and emotional pain.

"Whether you want to be a better salesperson or a happier human being, getting to know the 'real you' is a good place to start. It is difficult to become a top performing salesperson if you have your head in the clouds and are confused as to who you are."

"Throughout the course of a lifetime," I said, "people develop ways of thinking about and seeing themselves. Every person has an image of himself or herself. The question is does your interpretation of your image match up with who you really are?"

"Remember those amusement parks 'fun houses' with the distorting mirrors? Those mirrors twisted our view of anything we put in front of them. They made us look tall or short or fat or thin, and it was fun because we knew it wasn't real.

But many of us have these distorting mirrors functioning in our heads, and they aren't helpful at all, because we believe the images they show. Our internal thought mirrors distort beliefs that twist our view of ourselves and of everything around us."

A well-dressed man in the back of the room raised his hand. I asked his name; he stood and in a raspy voice said, "Bob Lewinski." He went on, "This is an important topic for me. I'd like to share my thoughts with the group."

With a sense of anticipation, I said, "Please do so."

"I can tell you from personal experience it's never a good idea to sacrifice your integrity, and it is never a good idea to lose touch with the truth. If you want to become the best version of yourself, you always have to know what's genuine and true."

"Just as lying to others will cause you to lose their trust, so does lying to yourself compromise your own trust and confidence. To know yourself in a world that is constantly trying to make you someone else will help you get a step closer to your own goals."

I thanked Bob for his remarks and continued.

"You can numb your pain by distorting your self-perception, but an honest understanding of who you are is integral to your success. A disregard for objectivity will derail you from achieving your goals and dreams."

Whether overcoming emotional challenges like fear, rejection, or anxiety, or sales issues such as establishing trust, earning credibility, or closing sales, it requires we push truthful, honest and rational beliefs, through our brains.

Jenna responded with a nod that compelled me to add:

"A word of warning. Self-deception is a thinking pattern that will undermine your success. It is holding on to a belief despite strong evidence to the contrary. It is the process of denying or rationalizing away an opposing viewpoint or logical argument."

"When someone deceives you, he or she knows the truth about something and deliberately tries to conceal it from you. They may do this by telling you outright lies or by misleading you. But there is a different kind of deception that is more harmful. It comes from within and involves choosing to believe your own lies, often for self-serving or self-flattering reasons.

"I discovered long ago that ordinary salespeople live in a fantasy world of dreams and illusion. In their fairy-tale world, they convince themselves they are investing adequately in the prospecting process. They fully believe that they are going to reach their sales goals, right up until the final day of the year. They'll swear they're asking for referrals and talking to top-level decision-makers, but in most cases...(I shrugged), they're not. These ordinary salespeople are experts in self-deception.

"We all know that smoking kills but a smoker will tell himself or herself that most likely it won't happen to them, you lie to yourself and indeed convince yourself that it's fine to smoke. You know it kills but it will be someone else. I bet you can think of dozens of times you have said something like this to yourself at some time in your life.

"We delight in telling others the truth about them, but how many of you have a difficult time facing the truth about yourself? Beryl Markham wrote in *West with the Night*, 'You can live a lifetime and, at the end of it, know more about other people than you do about yourself.'

"For example, I knew a salesman who I'll call Eric, who used self-deception as a technique to avoid having to acknowledge his less than satisfactory sales performance. He believed he was a top performing salesperson. Yet he never invested any time figuring out why he wasn't reaching his sales quota.

"Eric wasn't honest with himself and for self-serving purposes decided to believe his own wishful thinking. Adlai Stevenson, an American politician and statesman, said, 'The cruelest lies are often told in silence.' "When faced with an inconsistency between his performance and protecting his self-image, Eric silently lied to himself. He rationalized by projecting qualities onto himself that were not there

"Eric's view of his own skills went far beyond his actual ability to close the sale. He believed what he wanted to believe rather than what was true."

There's a part of the human psyche that tends to accept that which is repeatedly put into the mind. As a result, the peddler of lies very often reaches a point where he/she believes that his/her lies are actually the truth.

I drew the silhouettes of three people on the board. "That leads to what the American philosopher and psychologist William James said:

"Whenever two people meet there are really six people present. Each person as they see themselves, each as the other sees them and each as they really are.'"

I surveyed the room. "Lying to yourself is an easy thing to do. In fact, in some situations, it's easier to lie than to be honest. However, if you lie to yourself often enough, you'll begin to believe the lies. If you believe your lies, eventually the lies tears at your heart and stunt your growth.

If you've been living under a cloud of delusional thinking, it's time to shine a bright light on the dirty secrets of your inner mind."

In the second session of the morning, I shined that bright light with Principle Twenty: Let Go of the Need to be Liked.

Key Principle # 20

Let Go of the Need to be Liked

I asked, "Who here wants to be liked?"

Everyone raised a hand. So did I.

"So it's unanimous," I said.

"For some reason, we all like to be liked. No revelation there. It's how we're wired. We hate it when people don't like us – even people we don't really know. Some of us will do almost anything to be liked. We love to please, even at the expense of our own happiness, values, beliefs and standards. We compromise ourselves a hundred ways and turn ourselves inside-out trying to make others like us.

"All of us would rather be liked than disliked. And it's okay to feel that way--as long as it's not obsessive.

"The problem is," I explained, "I see too many salespeople over-delivering, under-pricing, and giving away too much for free, all in the name of 'pleasing' the client. Educating prospects and providing good customer service are desirable, but as sales professionals, we've got to draw a line between service and servitude."

Sherman Jackson stepped forward to address the room. "Wanting the approval of other people is a natural human condition. We all like the occasional stroke and positive affirmations from others. But do you have the need to be liked? If you look to others to validate you, provide reassurance, and reinforce your worth, sales might not be the best career for you."

I added, "The need to be liked is a mind set that arises from a need to feel that you have value. The underlying assumption is 'I am worthless if someone doesn't like me.' When you accept that not everyone is going to like you, then you can stop trying so hard to please everyone.

"The more worried you are about what other people think of you, the less freedom you will have. Because most people want to please, they try to become what they believe others expect, even if it means forcing themselves to be the kind of person they aren't.

"For the past ten years, we've hear a lot of talk about identity theft when someone steals your social security number and pretends to be you. But the more disturbing form of identity theft is to lose your own identity by denying the real you.

"One of the most freeing things we can learn in our lives is that it is okay to NOT be liked by everyone. Life isn't always fair and even though you may very well be a fantastic human being, some people will find a reason to dislike you no matter what you do.

"Everyone wants to be liked. It's a part of being human. We all need to know we are noticed and appreciated and our efforts are recognized. But some salespeople have an obsession with being liked. I describe this as the need to-be-liked syndrome and it is a recipe for failure." I stood beside the white board. **"Tell me the characteristics of salespeople who have a need to be liked."**

I wrote as the salespeople replied:

"Depend on others to give them a sense of self-worth."

"Avoid conflict."

"Always put others before themselves."

"Work hard to keep the peace at any price."

"Have a problem letting others know how they think and feel."

"Lack self-confidence."

"Have a tendency to shy away from the truth."

"Fear rejection."

Great responses. I said, "If you are a people-pleaser, you feel controlled by a need to please others, and you're always seeking approval from others. But rather than getting your 'affection' from customers, get it at home, and maintain healthy boundaries with your customers.

"Prospects and customers take advantage of salespeople who have a need to be liked by implying that greater effort is needed to gain their approval. They demand more of your time, energy and resources. They demand bigger discounts, more service, and better quality. They enjoy the authority they have and become condescending and unreasonable in their demands."

"In your interactions with others, if your niceness prevents you from sharing what makes you happy, upset, or disappointed, then there is little chance of building an authentic relationship.

"The more you identify with being nice, instead of being real, the more you'll find yourself plagued by insecurities and irrational fears. Nearly all the salespeople I've met who suffer from the 'need-to-be-liked' syndrome are naturally caring individuals. But because of their need to be accepted and liked, they sacrifice their ability to be genuine."

William Daniels raised his hand. "So if you're in a position where you feel the 'need' to be liked, no matter what a client or prospect does, should that be the time to explore inside yourself and figure out why?"

"Let me comment with this example," I replied. "I once worked with a salesman named Kevin. During my coaching session with him, I discovered his sales numbers were plummeting because he was more interested in pleasing people than in closing sales.

"He explained himself by saying, 'I've been in sales for nine years. When I started in sales, I didn't need prospects to like me. I knew my job was to sell, and I didn't let anything get in the way of that goal. During the past two years, that changed. Now I have a difficult time not taking things personally. When I'm in front of a prospect, I worry about what I do and what I say. I'm afraid I might offend the prospect, so I don't ask the important questions. I'm more concerned with how prospects think about me than I am with helping them achieve their business goals.'

"Kevin's desire to be liked caused him to make popular decisions rather than professional decisions. Selling can't be a popularity contest. Problems occur when salespeople value being liked to such an extent that they make poor decisions.

"Sales champions are not trying to build friendships and they will not be influenced to digress from their goals. Although they will develop friendships and are likable people, they do not misunderstand their real purpose. Their objective is not to win friends and to be liked; rather it's to establish rapport, credibility and trust.

"Sales champions are respected, credible, and good problem solvers. Being everyone's best friend isn't a high priority."

William raised his hand again. "So the question is, how to avoid that trap?"

"That's leads us to..." I wrote on the board, "Principle Twenty-one: Eliminate Submissive Behavior."

Key Lessons

- Excuse-making is one of the most destructive barriers to self-improvement and self-realization. You can make excuses but they won't help you live a more fulfilling or successful life.

- A salesperson that makes excuses and refuses to accept responsibility has little chance for improvement.

- I learned long ago that it is easier to a failure into a success than it is to turn an excuse into an opportunity.

- Human beings are pros at lying to themselves. Many people navigate through life with blinders over their eyes because they feel it's easier to avoid the truth than facing it.

- Just as lying to others will cause you to lose their trust, so does lying to yourself compromise your own trust.

- Lying to yourself is an easy thing to do. In fact, in some situations, it's easier to lie than to be honest. However, if you lie to yourself often enough, you'll begin to believe the lies.

- When you accept that not everyone is going to like you, then you can stop trying so hard to please everyone.

- Sales champions are respected, credible, and good problem solvers. Being everyone's best friend isn't a high priority.

- If you look to others to validate you, provide assurance, and reinforce your worth, sales might not be the best career for you.

Key Principle # 21

Eliminate Submissive Behavior

I explained, "Sometimes the toughest thing about feelings and opinions is sharing them with our prospects and customers. Maybe you believe your feelings and opinions aren't good or important enough. For many salespeople this self-defeating belief is hard-wired in their brain. They think, 'What I have to say isn't important. I'm not important.' Over time, this submissive thinking prevents them from performing at a higher level.

"Salespeople that are submissive see themselves as insignificant and lacking credibility. The core assumption of submissive behavior is that you are inferior to others and hence that others have greater rights and more valid truths than you.

"The fact that some salespeople permit others to define their success and failure makes them victims of other people's views. And because of that, these people often believe they are limited and cannot expect much success and happiness in their lives.

"Submissive people deprive themselves of voicing their opinions and as a result, they feel powerless. The result of submissive behavior is that you get little of what you want while losing the respect of other people.

"If you value yourself and trust your own feelings, you will make decisions based on your core values and not simply to please someone else. When this transformation takes place, others will respect and trust you.

"This 'I'll do anything' to make a sale' mentality creates an unhealthy situation in which salespeople do whatever it takes to satisfy the other party's wishes. Salespeople with these behavior patterns put themselves at risk of being used and taken for granted, which leads to stress, guilt, and poor sales performance. Which translates to..." I rubbed my fingertips together. "A lack of sales."

The salespeople laughed to acknowledge the truth of what I'd said.

"Here's another example," I continued. "Mary has been in sales for seven years and has a substantial number of clients. Her customers love her because she does everything they ask her to do. Her client retention rate is good, but when you analyze the profitability of her business, you discover her profit margins are well below where they should be. Because of her subservient attitude, she discounts her prices too much and leaves lots of money on the table.

"Mary isn't effectively managing her daily activities because she's jumping through hoops for her clients. As a result, she doesn't have time to prospect for new clients, which causes her anxiety. She's spending more time in the office working on customer service issues and less time at home with her family.

"During my conversation with Mary, she explained how some of her clients have treated her. She said, 'They apply pressure on me to conform to their desires and wishes. I didn't want to get them upset, so, I camouflaged my feelings and didn't speak up. This portrayed me as weak, inadequate, and helpless.'"

I said, "It is difficult to develop professional business relationships when you carry around unexpressed feelings. Suppressing feelings can be detrimental to your self-confidence. If done often enough, it will imprison you emotionally and create barriers between you and other people.

"To eliminate her self-defeating behavior, Mary refocused her thinking--she stopped second-guessing herself,--took ownership of her 'real feelings' and began to express how she felt.

"Mary later told me, 'Speaking the truth can be uncomfortable but when I put my foot down with disrespectful clients, my confidence shot through the roof. In addition, I got what I was after far more often. I learned it is far better to feel uncomfortable saying how you feel, than to experience the pain of concealing your feelings.'"

"To what extent do you find yourself behaving in a subservient way in your everyday life? Why are you doing it? What results are you getting for doing it? What do you think would happen if you spoke up like Mary and said what you really feel?"

I paused to write on the board. *Respect.*

"The lesson here is: To gain the respect of others, you first must believe you deserve respect. And the more respect you have for yourself, the more respect others will have for you."

"To get command of your submissive habits, begin by observing your behavior closely when you are with other. Only by bringing your submissive behavior to the forefront of your mind will you be able to get command of them and change them."

I projected the following questions on the screen for everyone to see.

"Do you agree that you are wrong even though you know that you are right?"

"Do you tend to go along with others without thinking through whether it makes sense to do so?"

"Do you do things because other people are doing them, rather than because you want to?"

"Do you let others 'put-you-down' without defending yourself?"

"Do you listen quietly if people in authority say unpleasant things about you?"

"Do you avoid direct eye contact?"

"So we arrive at the final topic for the morning, Principle Twenty-two: Stop Walking on Eggshells."

Key Principle # 22

Stop Walking on Eggshells

Sherman spoke up. "This is a great topic. Have you ever wondered why some salespeople always seem to get what they want while others rarely do? How do they do it? They know how to assert themselves."

William said, "I have trouble saying no, even when I know I should."

David McDonald joined in. "What about when I feel prospects and customers are taking advantage of me?"

"These concerns are legitimate and I'm glad you brought them up," I replied. "What they may indicate is a lack of assertiveness."

I wrote *Assertive* on the board. "What does it mean to be assertive? Let's start by defining what it is not. Being assertive does not mean being aggressive, hostile, threatening, demanding, or sarcastic. Assertiveness differs from aggression because standing up for yourself does not trespass on the rights of others.

"Being assertive is standing up for yourself and expressing your thoughts, feelings and beliefs in a direct, honest and appropriate way that does not infringe upon another person's rights. It is neither passive nor aggressive. And it is motivated neither by fear nor by anger.

"Assertiveness is about choosing to tell the truth to someone who needs to hear it, rather than tucking it away. Assertiveness is about stating clearly what you want without either retreating into a shell or bullying others.

"Assertiveness is the ability to honestly express your opinions and feelings, without undue anxiety, in a way that *doesn't infringe on the rights of others*. Being assertive is communicating the idea that your needs, wants and feelings are neither more nor less important than those of other people. The goal of assertion is to get and give respect and to expect fairness in return.

"Many salespeople are taught to defer to prospects' and customers' wants and needs. As a matter of fact, there is an unwritten rule when it comes to working with customers, - Most of us have this rule hard-wired into our heads."

I asked the salespeople: "What's the unwritten rule when working with customers?"

The salespeople answered in chorus, "The customer is always right."

Unfortunately, this generalization isn't helping salespeople feel as if they can speak-up and assert themselves. The result, salespeople get stressed out, lose power, happiness and overall sense of well being.

David McDonald spoke-up, "When a customer or prospect takes advantage of you, it's like your insides feel simultaneously numb and sick, like there's a knife being twisted in your stomach."

I replied, "The customer is important, but he's not always right. It's not that we shouldn't listen to customers or place special emphasis on understanding their wants and needs, concerns and complaints. It's that we must do so with discernment. Sometimes the customer is just plain wrong and you may have to help him discover that."

While it's important to serve other people, many salespeople have the belief, "What makes me important is taking care of others." That belief will have you put others first and not do what you should do to take care of yourself.

"Have you noticed that when you don't take care of your own physical and emotional needs,--you are less able to take care of others, and your ability to handle challenging situations is compromised?

"We've all heard the familiar mantra of the airline flight attendants during their pre-flight instructions," '...make sure to put the oxygen mask on yourself first before attempting to help someone else put on theirs.'" This demonstrates the importance of strengthening our own life skills before we can effectively serve others.

"Salespeople who avoid being assertive do so because they're afraid of upsetting others. However, in their attempt not to hurt someone else's feelings, they harbor feelings of disappointment and anger toward those who disrespect them.

"Self-improvement begins with the elimination of unassertive behaviors, gestures and speech patterns. Steer clear of passive behaviors such as avoiding eye contact, speaking too softly, being indecisive, or minimizing the importance of your needs and wants. Poor eye contact, slouching, nervous gestures and other non assertive behaviors can convince others that what we have to say can be safely ignored.

"Passive communication involves the inability or unwillingness to express thoughts and feelings. Passive salespeople often do things they don't want to do or make excuses to avoid saying how they really feel. Often, they are afraid to express themselves due to a fear of conflict. In an effort to avoid disagreement, they stay silent rather than honestly speak about what upsets them. Ultimately, their anger gets leaked out rather than worked out.

"Passive salespeople are controlled by fear. They don't tell others how they feel about something, especially if their opinions differ. The passive message is, 'My feelings don't matter - only yours do. My thoughts aren't important – yours are the only ones worth listening to. I'm not important because I am a salesperson--you are superior because you're the buyer.' What their self-talk is saying is, 'I don't count! So go ahead and take advantage of me.'

"Passive salespeople are not committed to their own beliefs and are more likely to allow others to infringe on their rights than to stand up and speak out."

Jenna asked, "Can you give some examples of passive behavior?"

"Sure I can." I read from page 19 in the handout.

"There's no use in opposing them because they are more powerful than I am."

"No one cares about how I feel."

"It's important for people to like me and I say anything just so long as they like me."

"I hide my feelings well from others."

"My feelings don't count. It's better to ignore my feelings than upset another person."

I raised my voice a notch to emphasize what I was about to say. "A passive attitude will not help you achieve success and happiness in your life. Indeed, one of the most powerful and energizing things you can do is to stop walking on eggshells. You do that by standing up for yourself from a position of strength, not fear."

"We moved to the next Key Principle Twenty-three: Put Your Goals in Writing."

Key Principle # 23

Put Your Goals in Writing

We broke for lunch and afterwards, returned to the classroom. I'd begin with Principle Twenty-three: Put Your Goals in Writing, and used this quote from Brian Tracy to herald the discussion:

"An average person with average talent, ambition and education can outstrip the most brilliant genius in our society, if that person has clear, focused goals and works on them every day."

I looked across the room. "If I had to guess, I'd be willing to bet that you want to achieve more this year than you did last year, right? But how many of you actually developed an action plan that will help you realize your goals?

"At another sales seminar, I had asked how many attendees had their sales goals in writing. Their answers surprised me, but not in a good way. Of the 135 salespeople present, only five admitted to writing down their goals. The rest either didn't have goals or didn't remember them.

"In Lewis Carroll's classic story, *Alice's Adventures in Wonderland,* Alice arrived at an intersection and was unsure which road to take. She asked the Cheshire cat which route she should follow and he said, 'That will depend on where you are going!' Alice replied that she did not know where she was going, so the cat said, 'Then it doesn't really matter which road you take.' This story demonstrates that without a goal, you are going to wander aimlessly.

"In our journey to greater success, what do we need to do first?"

William Daniels answered, "Define your goals."

"Next?" I pressed the room.

"Set a course," Jenna Gomez said.

David McDonald added, "Follow the directions on how to get there."

"Very good," I replied. "Throughout history, much has been written on the importance of goal setting. In his epic work, *The Dynamic Laws of Success*, Napoleon Hill interviewed many of the most successful men and women of his day and found that the common thread among these top achievers was their commitment to setting and executing their goal plans."

This was Sherman Jackson's cue to comment. "I remember reading about a Yale University study conducted in 1953 that revealed information about goal setting. By studying the graduating class of 1953, the authors found that of all the graduating seniors, only three percent had written goals and plans to achieve them. They found that these three percent-- the goal-setters--earned more than the other 97 percent."

"A great example," I said. "Despite the importance we place on achieving goals, it never ceases to amaze me how many salespeople fall short each year."

I wrote the number 95 on the board. "About 95 percent of the salespeople I've met understand why setting a goal is important, and know what types of goals they should set. I also discovered that 70 percent of salespeople understand the proper way to structure a goal plan, such as by using the acronym SMART (specific, measurable, attainable, realistic and timely). But last year up to 50 percent of business-to-business sales reps failed to achieve their goals. Why?"

Jenna raised her hand. "Because they haven't written a plan?"

"That's half right," I replied. "Very few salespeople understand what they need to do on a daily basis to achieve their goals. And those that do aren't disciplined to follow through."

Jenna had kept her hand raised. "So where do you begin?"

I readied my marker. "By applying these proven goal-setting ideas."

I jotted on the white board:

1. Relax and brainstorm your personal and career goals. Be creative and write down all your dreams and desires.
2. Prioritize your goals and put them in writing.
3. Define your sales and production goals and make them quantifiable. For example: I want to close $70,000 in new business and $300,000 in repeat business.
4. Break down your "high-pay" "activities (activities that help you reach your goals) in daily, weekly, monthly, quarterly and yearly goals.
5. Block uninterrupted work time in your calendar to follow your plan. Force yourself to remain focused and avoid distractions. Discipline is one of the keys to reaching your goals.
6. Keep accurate records. Record your progress every day and review your results regularly.
7. Share your goals with others. Studies show that salespeople who share their goals with team members are more likely to achieve them.

I turned from the board. "Does everyone have these?"

Deciding on your goals is one of the first steps in creating your success program. And yet, creating goals means absolutely nothing unless you commit 100 percent to achieving your goals.

The salespeople were busy putting my comments in their notebooks and computers.

When they were done, I erased the white board to signal we were moving on to the next section, which I announced as, "Now to Principle Twenty-four: Live Your Purpose."

Key Lessons

- If you value yourself and trust your own feelings, you will make decisions based on your core values and not simply to please someone else. When this transformation takes place, others will respect and trust you.

- To gain the respect of others, you first must believe you deserve respect. And the more respect you have for yourself, the more respect others will have for you.

- Self-improvement begins with the elimination of unassertive behaviors, gestures and speech patterns.

- Passive salespeople are not committed to their own beliefs and are more likely to allow others to infringe on their rights than to stand up and speak out.

- An average person with average talent, ambition and education can outstrip the most brilliant genius in our society, if that person has clear, focused goals and acts on them every day.

- There are many ways to determine what's most important. If you know yourself well, begin by focusing on your strengths - the things that make the best use of your skills.

- If you want to achieve great things, you need to have great plans. Deciding on your goals is one of the first steps in creating your success program. And yet, creating goals means absolutely nothing unless you commit 100 percent to achieving them.

Key Principle # 24

Live Your Purpose

I asked the salespeople to turn to page 29 in their handout, and I read: "Oprah Winfrey said, 'You may think that real work is doing your job, but the real work is finding what you're supposed to do with your life!'

"Over the years, as I have watched, listened to and studied successful salespeople, I discovered a common thread. They know why they're here. Knowing their purpose in life gives them clarity, stability and a track to run on.

"Someone once said there are two great days in our lives – the day we are born and the day we discover why.

"Highly successful people have discovered their *why.*"

Have you ever stopped to think about what you really want out of your career and your life? Many people haven't. And if you don't know what you really want, chances are you're not going to get it.

"Many of the people I've met admitted they came late to the realization of what really matters in their lives. Usually they were awakened because of a crisis. An illness, a job loss, a death, or some other event that shook them to the core and forced them to examine what really mattered.

"One of the hardest and most fearful times of my life was the day my doctor told me I suffered a heart attack. It was June 2009. Prior to my heart attack, my mother and father had just passed away. It was a challenging time. There was so much going on and so much uncertainty in my life. Now, when I look back, although it was a terribly trying time, I realize it was also an enormous gift that was instrumental in waking me up and caused me to enter into a kind of inner reflection, an inner awakening.

As shaken as I was to lose my parents and suffer a heart attack, those experiences gave me resilience and strength to help figure out the meaning in my life."

"When you're young, you have this seemingly endless future ahead of you. As I got older, I realized that life is delicate, fragile and short, I made better choices about how I invested my time and what was important. Intellectually, I understood that earlier, but you know it and feel it much more as you get older."

"I became curious about the effects of this inspiration. After sitting down and pondering over this, the answer hit me like a ton of bricks. I came across a very simple, yet elegant understanding for what was happening: I was aligning myself with my purpose in life."

"The big epiphany for me is that good health and success isn't about me. It's about the people I love. The people I care about. The people who depend on me at home and work."

I wrote on the board as I said, "*My why.*"

The words seemed to strike a chord in the audience and I could see the salespeople shift in their seats to focus their attention.

I explained, "Your purpose is what you feel compelled to accomplish. This gives meaning and direction to your life. Your purpose guides your beliefs and your behavior. It empowers you to make daily decisions that are consistent with your values and goals."

Having a purpose is not a privilege for the few. It is a right and power you are born with. When you find your purpose in life, things naturally fall into place, and you feel like you're no longer paddling against the current.

If you lose track of your purpose, and get caught in the treadmill of everyday life, you risk living a life full of regret. Henry David Thoreau said, "Many men go fishing all of their lives without knowing that it is not fish that they are after."

Margaret Bambery, a salesperson sitting in the front row, raised her hand. "How do you discover your real purpose in life? I'm not talking about your job, your daily responsibilities, or even your long-term goals. I mean the reason you exist?"

"Start by asking yourself these three questions."

I wrote on the board:

What is it that you truly love to do?

What is the legacy you most want to leave for others?

What makes your life worth living?

When you discover the answers to these questions, you will feel them resonate deep within you. When that happens, you'll know you're closer to identifying your true purpose.

William Marsten, a prominent psychologist, asked 3,000 people, "What have you to live for?" Ninety-four percent said they had no definite purpose for their lives. "Fear not that thy life shall come to an end, but rather fear that it shall never have a beginning," was the advice of English writer and theologian, Cardinal John Henry Newman.

Sherman asked, "How exactly are you supposed to define your purpose? Are you simply supposed to know it and squeeze it out of your brain like a sponge?"

Not exactly. "If you want to define your purpose, there is one sure path to get you there. Connect with your true purpose, instead of a lesser purpose.

"When you only look to fulfill your personal wants and needs, it's easy to lose your way and separate yourself from your true purpose in life, leaving you feeling like you're going nowhere."

Sherman asked, "How does this happen?"

You have choices in life. You can "default" into "false or lesser purposes" based in your self-serving ego, *or* direct your life from your true purpose, which originates in your heart and soul.

The most purposeful people in the world invest their time doing what they love. Bill Gates loves computers, Oprah loves helping, and Edison loved to invent. What do you love? Is it reading, writing, playing sports, painting, selling, playing the piano, cooking, gardening? Whatever you love is probably directly related to your purpose.

I panned the room of salespeople. "People wonder what their lives are all about, hoping their purpose will flash before them like a bolt of lightning. Reflection is necessary, but simply thinking about your purpose is only the first step.

"You're not going to figure it out through theory and speculation. You learn what you want from life by living life. Trial and error. Success and failure. These are the experiences that will bring you closer to understanding what it is you want to get out of life."

The happiest, most successful people do more than simply figure out what they want. They take time to learn the skills they need to make sure they get the things they want.

I jotted on the board. *Thinking--> Action*"

"Once you've identified your overall purpose, the next step is to turn that purpose into achievable goals and actions. Remember, action produces results!"

I explained, "Without a purpose, I never would have found the strength to leave a successful 12-year, career in the newspaper and publishing business, to pursue my dreams and seize the opportunity to help develop, motivate and coach salespeople.

"I didn't leave because someone offered me lots of money. As a matter of fact, the sales training company I went to work for offered me no salary and no health insurance for my family. There wasn't any signing bonus, expense account, or 401K program. It was a straight commission job."

I drew a heart on the board. "I took a risk, but when your heart speaks and you find the courage to act, you live with a sense of contentment and knowledge knowing you are who you want to be."

"Gradually, I came into my present view of success, which is that when you get up in the morning you're really glad to be alive – that you're so absorbed with what you do you don't know if it's work or play. That what you're doing is not only fulfilling to you, but also brings a tremendous good to a greater community.

You have a sense of purpose. Yes,' I'm doing exactly what I was put here to do and what I'm doing is a benefit to a host of people. And it's my privilege to be in such a position where I am of service.' If you're in that situation, where you're grateful to be given the opportunity to do what you enjoy doing, then you're living your dream."

I wrote: *Live Your Purpose*.

"Of all pursuits, the quest to 'live your purpose' will take you higher than any other."

Key Principle # 25

Don't Settle for Mediocrity

That evening, when I returned to my hotel room, the message light on my room phone was blinking. I had a message from Roger Unger, Sherman Jackson's Vice-President of Sales, giving me his private number and asking that I call him back right away, which I did.

He answered and after a gracious exchange of greetings, informed me of what he wanted to discuss.

"We've got an excellent sales team, the best in the business. Still, I feel that as a group, we're not firing on all cylinders. Some of our people are not meeting expectations. Anywhere else, they'd be top-notch, but at Palisades Global Mutual, we've got high standards to maintain. Frankly, in our sales environment, the performance of a few of our people can be considered mediocre."

"I understand," I replied. "In any group, you've always got some degree of separation. Everyone may consider themselves champions, but that doesn't mean everyone is going to finish in first place. Mediocrity is a topic I'm going to discuss."

"Thanks," replied Roger. "It can be a delicate subject but one that we have to address."

The following morning, I continued by writing on the white board, "Principle Twenty-five: Don't Settle for Mediocrity."

I looked over the room and nodded to recognize Roger. I said, "For the past 15 years, I've been working with business owners, presidents of companies, and salespeople to help them realize their goals and improve their business results.

"When people ask what I do, I tell them I have one of the best jobs anyone could ever dream of. Imagine waking up every morning and going to work with one goal: helping people achieve greater success. That's what I do." I capped that remark with a smile.

"You would think that helping people maximize their potential would be an easy assignment. It's not. Here's the reason. It is remarkable how stubborn people interested in self-improvement can be. They say that they want to improve themselves, but at the same time they want to defend that what they're thinking and doing are already right. They say they want to become successful, but in truth, most remain in their comfort zone and settle for mediocrity.

"No one likes to think of themselves as being mediocre. However, the reality is that many people seem content with just getting by…doing just enough to keep their heads above water."

I wrote *Mediocrity* on the board and underlined it in red. "To settle for mediocrity simply means you are willing to live beneath your abilities.

Regrettably, many salespeople have no motivation to succeed, instead choosing lives of desperation that are dull, drab and uneventful, never realizing that nothing extraordinary gets accomplished by mediocre performance.

"Salespeople are not born mediocre. So what's fueling the mediocre train that hundreds of thousands ride? What is it that explains the excellent performance of some salespeople and the lack of effort in others?" In a slightly elevated voice I said, "It's mediocre thinking."

How much time do you devote to mediocre thinking? When people ask you how you are, do you automatically respond with "not bad," "pretty good," "I've been better," or just "okay?" Many people are conditioned to respond in mediocre terms instead of thinking about what they're saying and considering alternative responses.

Roger Unger, Vice President of Sales, stood before the audience and with the determination of a battalion commander said, "We must overcome the notion that it's okay to aspire to be average. Settling to be average robs us of the opportunity to be extraordinary and forces us to settle for mediocrity."

I followed with, "All that is necessary for mediocrity to win out is that good salespeople do nothing extraordinary." The great football coach Vince Lombardi said, "The quality of a person's life is in direct proportion to their commitment to excellence, regardless of their chosen field of endeavor."

I added, "Just as excellence is a state of mind, mediocrity is too. It is a mind set, and attitude, a way of thinking. If you want to end the mediocrity in your life, you must wipe out the thinking that perpetuate it."

Just then, William Daniels stopped me. He said in a rather agitated tone of voice, "Why are you lecturing us about mediocrity? We are one of the most successful sales teams in our industry. You're talking to a group of top performers."

"I'm not suggesting that anyone here is mediocre. However, if Mr. Jackson thought everyone in this room reached their highest level of achievement, we wouldn't be here."

Sherman Jackson looked up and said, "Robert Louis Stevenson said it more than a hundred years ago: 'To become what we are capable of becoming is the only end in life.' We are all on a lifetime journey where success is ultimately defined by, and anchored in, living up to our full potential. It is an oxymoron to think of someone having found success if they haven't reached their highest level of personal achievement."

Sherman continued. "What are you really celebrating as success? What do you mean when you say you're a top performer? More often than not, when salespeople think of themselves as top performers they're comparing themselves and their results to salespeople who aren't performing very well," He paused for a moment and took a deep breath. "Ask yourself – have you reached your highest level of performance based on your abilities? If you haven't, are you really a top performer?"

To answer the question, I offered this quote, "The great basketball coach, John Wooden said it best: 'Don't measure yourself by what you've accomplished, but rather by what you should have accomplished with your abilities.'

"Face it; you are amazing creations, filled with incredible potential. Dr. William James, the cofounder of the Mayo Clinic, said, 'Even the most effective humans utilize less than 10 percent of their mental capacity.' The Brain Research Institute at the University of California at Los Angeles has concluded that the creative potential of the human brain may be infinite."

Sherman spoke up, "If each of you were able to improve your sales performance by just 10 percent, how much more successful would each of you be? How many more clients would you have? How much more money would you be earning?"

American business writer Lou Vickery believes: "Nothing average ever stood as a monument of progress. When progress is looking for a partner it doesn't turn to those who believe that they are only average. It turns instead to those who are forever searching and striving to become the best they possibly can. If we seek the average level, we cannot hope to achieve a higher level of success. Our only hope is to avoid being a failure."

I stated, "Don't surrender to one of our greatest enemies: mediocrity. Whatever you choose as your work, do it with excellence. Live your life and do your work in the embodiment of excellence, otherwise mediocrity will show up in its place."

I erased *Mediocrity*, replaced it with *Excellence* and moved on to "Principle Twenty-six: Good Isn't Good Enough."

Key Principle # 26

Good Isn't Good Enough

"As *New York Times* columnist and Pulitzer Prize winning author Thomas Friedman points out," I noted, "globalization has leveled the competitive field; a new idea can have dozens of competitors worldwide within months. With this as a backdrop, the 'good enough' syndrome no longer cuts it, and the premium on excellence is higher than ever.

"In business it's clear that the standards of performance will continue to rise more than they have in the past, thus increasing the value of excellence.

"But it isn't just companies that have to keep kicking up their performance more than they ever did before. It's each of us individually. The pressure on salespeople to keep improving has never been greater.

"There was a time when being a good salesperson meant you were on top or at least near the top of your field. If your product or service was good, you would attract customers. If you were good at selling, you could make a decent living.

"Today, however, with advances being made at increasing speeds - rising competition, and information readily available to anyone with Internet access, the days of trying to stay ahead by just being good are gone. Being good, isn't good enough.

"When you let yourself do just enough to get by, that's all you'll ever do. You'll just get by for the rest of your life. All the great things in the world happen when you stop treading water and strive for something better."

If this world is inhabited by those who do just an average job, then we have an average world. If however, the standard in the world is one of excellence – one where we discover and live our unique abilities

– then we create a far better world.

My high school football coach, Silvio Cella, kicked off every football season with the same speech, "I won't accept anything less than the best from my players. Don't be content with being good enough because good enough is just about as close to the bottom as it is to the top." He made it perfectly clear, "Performing as an average football player is the equivalent to performing as a loser."

Marker in hand, I stood in front of the white board. "Now you answer. **Good enough isn't good enough because...**"

David McDonald replied, "Someone will always do better and it's your fault they're getting ahead instead of you."

Jenna Gomez spoke next, "You'll always wonder 'what if?'"

William Daniels said, "You'll have many regrets." He added, "And you'll set the wrong example for everyone around you."

David again contributed, "No one remembers people who just get by."

I jotted their comments. "The truth is salespeople have little choice; they either improve or they're forced to choose a different career." I advise all my clients, "'If you are going to compete in the sales arena, play hard and give-it-your-best effort, or don't play at all.'

"Think about this: "How much revenue does your company earn when you come in second? How much commission do you earn when your company comes in second? The answer to both questions is obvious, which is why it is absolutely crucial that you make every effort to be the best and come in first. Second best is good, but being the best is much better."

And now, to the next step. "Principle Twenty-seven: Push Past Your Limits."

Key Lessons

- Having a purpose is not a privilege for the few. It is a right and power you are born with.

- You may think that the 'real' work in life is doing your work, but the 'real' work is finding what you're suppose to do with your life.

- Your purpose is what you feel compelled to accomplish. It gives meaning and direction to your life.

- The most purposeful people in the world invest their time doing what they love.

- Most people say they want to be successful, but in truth, most remain in their comfort zone and settle for mediocrity.

- It is remarkable how stubborn people interested in self-improvement can be, They say that they want to improve themselves, but at the same time they want to defend that what they're thinking and doing are already right.

- Whatever you choose as your work, do it with excellence. Live your life and do your work in the embodiment of excellence, otherwise mediocrity will show up in its place.

- The days of trying to stay ahead by just being good are gone. Being good, isn't good enough.

- The truth is salespeople have little choice; they either improve or they're forced to choose a different career.

Key Principle # 27

Push Past Your Limits

No matter what innate talents and gifts you were born with, what family you were born into, the neighborhood you live in, your education and interpersonal skills, nothing will get you to where you want to be quicker than opening up your mind and *shifting your thinking.* Think about your past, your present, and your future. Ask yourself questions like…What am I capable of? What are my strengths? What excites me? Where do I want to be in 5 years, 10 years?

Get lost in your thought…it's one of the break-through factors in just about every success story.

To show this, I explained, "A few weeks ago, I was coaching a client that works for a large newspaper company who said, 'I know what I'm capable of and what I could become. I can see it, but it always seems just beyond my reach. I don't feel that I'm living up to my full potential.'

"I had asked her, 'Are you excited about your life? Or do you feel as if you merely exist? Are you moving with confidence toward a desired goal? Or do you feel as if you are drifting along from day to day without any sense of direction?'"

I said,"Every day, we have the option to live with passion, be open to possibility, and reach for the stars. We have the freedom to boldly live, laugh, and love."

I encouraged her, "Don't wait for permission. Begin today. Choose to be inspired and motivated enough, to live without limits. Get off the couch and do something extraordinary! Let go of your fear, get gutsy, and get going. I reminded her that circumstances improve when you make the effort to improve them."

I explained to the audience, **"If you want to reach your full potential, then you must face up to these three truths,"** and wrote:

1. "You have more potential within you than you realize."

2. "You likely have settled for the life you now live."

3. "Once you unlock your mind from self-limiting thoughts you can experience the talents and gifts you were given to live a happy and successful life."

Through the years, I have met countless salespeople who somehow along their journeys became complacent and content in their circumstances. They settled for what they believed was satisfactory. They turned their backs on their future and refused to seek more or pursue more.

Few people really know what their full potential is. And even fewer realize that discovering their potential allows them to achieve amazing things in every area of their lives.

Jenna spoke up, "How do you reach your full potential?"

You have to turn inward, toward your heart and soul. The journey begins with self-discovery and introspection, where you take a good, long look at yourself by...

1. Identifying your unique talents, interests and abilities.

2. Clarifying your purpose and goals.

3. Reviewing your life experiences.

4. Recognizing the person that you can become.

5. Revealing what is possible for you to achieve.

I wrote *Average* on the board, and above it, *Excel*. God didn't create you to be average. You were created to excel. You have everything you need to fulfill your destiny, and there is no limit to what you are capable of accomplishing.

"The greatest waste in human life is the difference between *what we are* and *what we are capable of becoming*. Settling for common is not what we're supposed to do."

I wrote *Thomas Edison* on the board. "We all know who he is.

Edison said, 'If we did all the things we are capable of doing, we would literally astound ourselves.' Whatever you want, you can have, if you want it badly enough and are willing to persist long enough in doing what others have done to achieve success.

"Consider the mighty oak tree. Its journey to greatness begins with a small seed. Of course, the seed has to go through a number of changes and stages of development in order to reach its full potential, but the potential is a constant: to become a great oak tree.

"Just like the seed of the mighty oak tree, there's treasure to be discovered, and it's within you. According to Mary Kay Ash, the founder of Mary Kay Cosmetics, 'The seed of greatness is inside all of us, however, I discovered that it takes a lot more than a seed to become a sales champion.'"

I turned to the room. "I believe that everyone has a seed of greatness on the inside of them. Greatness is within you. That is true whether you recognize it or not. It's true whether you affirm it or not. It's true whether you are focused on your personal development and personal growth or not."

"Greatness is inherently in you. Greatness is in everyone yet most people have no idea of what their greatness is, how to bring it to life or that it even exists. The truth is that you are a powerful person with immense power and natural ability."

I wrote the number 6 on the white board and said, **"If you want to discover your greatness follow these six steps:"**

1. Surround yourself with people who will empower you to reach your full potential!
2. Make a decision to believe in your greatness.
3. Minimize the negative story-telling and maximize the positive story-telling.
4. Exaggerate your successful and empowering experiences and minimize your dis empowering ones.
5. Find what you're great at and let everything else go.

6. Take your time and enjoy the journey.

I referred the salespeople to page 32 in their handout. "I'd like to share a story about an eagle's nest that rested on a mountainside. One day an earthquake rocked the mountain, causing one of the eagle eggs to roll down the slope to a chicken farm in the valley below.

"The chickens knew that they had to protect and care for the mysterious egg so an old hen volunteered for the job." I sketched an egg surrounded by chickens.

"One day in the middle of spring, the egg hatched, and a beautiful eagle was born." I erased the egg and replaced it with an eagle. "Sadly, the eagle was raised to believe he was a chicken. The eagle loved his home and family, but his spirit yearned for more. While foraging in the fields one day, the eagle looked up and noticed a group of eagles soaring in the skies. 'Oh,' the eagle cried, 'I wish I could soar like those birds.' The chickens laughed at him. 'You cannot soar with those birds. You are a chicken, and chickens do not soar.'

"The eagle continued staring at his real family up above, dreaming he could be with them. Each time the eagle let his dreams be known, the chickens told him it couldn't be done. Soon the eagle stopped dreaming and he lived the rest of his life as a lowly chicken."

I drew XX's over the eagle's eyes. The audience chuckled.

I asked, "The moral of the story?"

Jenna answered, "You become what you believe you are capable of becoming."

"Correct," I replied. "If your goal is to become a great salesperson, then follow your dreams and don't listen to the chickens. The big challenge of life is to become all that you have the potential of becoming."

Sherman added, "There's no question that there's fear associated with fulfilling your potential. But when you learn to recognize it, you also learn to cope with it, not repress it."

I walked to the board and wrote while I recited, "If you lived up to your full potential what would be happening then that isn't happening now?"

"Write down the three benefits of living up to your full potential."

I erased the board to progress to the next lesson. "We're now at Principle Twenty-eight: Visualize Greatness.

Key Principle # 28

Visualize Greatness

To quote Napoleon Hill, "All the breaks you need in life wait within your imagination. Imagination is the workshop of your mind, capable of turning mind energy into accomplishment and wealth."

"I wrote *Visualize.*

Every successful salesperson I've ever met had a vision. They knew clearly what they wanted to accomplish in their lives and they were able to visualize it in their mind.

The easiest thing you can do to attract greater success into your life and career is to visualize it. Star athletes use visualization all the time to improve their performances, so why shouldn't you use it to improve your sales results?

Often the only thing holding salespeople back from greater success is that they can't visualize themselves as being more successful. It may take years, but to experience greatness, you must first create a vision of greatness within your mind.

Once you visualize a new image, your thought process goes to work, searching for ways to bring new opportunities into your life. When we can imagine a goal, visualize taking the steps necessary to gain that goal, a part of the Limbic system of the brain called the Reticular Activating system takes over and we guides us to do what it takes to achieve the desired result. The Reticular Activating System is the attention center in the brain. It is the key to "turning on your brain," and seems to be the center of motivation.

In the movie The Secret Dr. Denis Waitley supported this idea with his findings from his "Visual Motor Rehearsal" research on Olympic athletes and astronauts in the Apollo program. "When you visualize then you materialize. The mind can't distinguish whether you're really doing it or whether it's just a (mental) practice. If you've been there in the mind you'll go there in the body."

"As your mental focus builds, you will find greater strength to influence and improve your performance by controlling and directing your thoughts and feelings.

"Visualizing success means creating clear pictures in your mind of having already achieved your goals. Stephen Covey, in his book The Seven Habits of Highly Successful People, called it 'begin at the end' thinking. When you know what the outcome looks like, it's easier to create the path that will get you there.

"The pictures in your mind strengthen your effort to grow into whatever it is you want to become. Therefore, in order to achieve a better life, you need to visualize a picture of a better you."

In Robert Cooper's book, *Get Out of Your Own Way,* he says, "Brain scans show that simply imagining a complex and compelling goal will actually fire the same neurons that will be required to actually achieve the goal."

"An Olympic swimmer once shared his secret for dealing with the uncertainty that sometimes afflicted him. 'Whenever I feel my commitment flagging,' he said, 'and I feel like I just can't swim another length of the pool, I take a few moments to myself. I sit down, take a few deep breaths, close my eyes, and visualize myself on the top step of the podium with a gold medal around my neck. I hear *The Star Spangled Banner*. I feel myself fighting back tears while our flag is raised.'"

I let the image sink in. "Isn't that a powerful vision?"

I asked everyone to turn to page 37 in their handout. "I love this quote by Paul J. Meyer: 'Whatever you vividly imagine, ardently desire, sincerely believe, and enthusiastically act upon must inevitably come to pass.'

"To succeed, you have to have a goal--a destination--in mind. Once you set your sights on where you are going, move toward that direction and have faith that you will get there.

"History is filled with examples of people who had a vision and went on to accomplish great things. All the great inventions of mankind were first visualized in someone's imagination. An architect sees the master plan in his head before he commits his ideas to the drawing board. Authors write stories in their imaginations before putting them on paper. Coaches visualize their teams outperforming the competition before the game begins."

I stood by the white board. **"Here are three steps for applying visualization."**

I wrote as I recited:

"1. Decide on specific goals you want to achieve. Pick goals you consider realistic. As you get better at visualization, add goals that are more challenging.

"2. Close your eyes and imagine yourself arriving at that goal. See it as already achieved.

"3. Make the pictures in your mind as clear and complete as possible with vivid details. For example: What color is your new vacation house? What does each room look like? What are you doing in the house? What sounds do you hear? Is it near a lake or next to a busy intersection?

"Often when people are not succeeding at something, it's because they habitually and perhaps unconsciously, visualize failure and negative situations. If you visualize failure in the forefront of your mind, you're done. You have to imagine yourself succeeding, which allows you to then move onto a path of success. The analogy that race car drivers use is, "Focus on the road, not on the wall."

I put the marker down. "If you want to achieve greater success, invest time each day visualizing excellence until it becomes so ingrained in your mind that you have no other option but to succeed."

Pay the Price

At the end of the day, Sherman Jackson, a few of his salespeople, and I went out for cocktails. We arranged ourselves around a table on the mezzanine of the bar with a view through the window. Outside, an evening drizzle covered the pavement with a glossy patina that reflected the bright lights of Times Square.

While we waited for our drinks, Sherman began the conversation. "One thing we have to emphasize during the training is the work necessary for success. You love quotes and I have a favorite of my own. It was Michelangelo who said, 'If people knew how hard I had to work to gain my mastery, it wouldn't seem so wonderful at all.'"

"That's what my next session is about," I said. "Principle Twenty-nine: Pay the Price.

"Behind every success is a story of education, training, practice, self-discipline, and sacrifice."

Sherman noted, "Here's a story about a former college athlete that resonates with me. Before Bill Bradley became a U.S. Senator from New Jersey, he was a great basketball player for the New York Knicks, and was inducted into the Basketball Hall of Fame. How did he manage to do so well at his sport? In his memoir, *Time Present, Time Past*, Bradley offers the following account of his training regimen: 'I stayed behind to practice after my teammates had left. My practice routine was to end by making 15 baskets in a row from each of the five spots on the floor.' If he missed a shot, he would start all over from the beginning."

Sherman looked about the table. "I want you to understand that if you want an extraordinary sales career, you must realize there is a price to pay."

"Which leads to this question," I added. "What does it mean to pay the price?"

William Daniels answered, "It means we must give up something to get something. Of course, if you don't know what the price is, you can't choose to pay it."

"That's correct," I replied. "I see examples of salespeople who want the results, without paying the price. The true rewards of sales come to those who actively go out and seek them. Seldom does success arrive at your door step. It's achieved by those salespeople who labor long and hard.

"There will always be sacrifice. You can't build a successful sales career without sacrifice. I know first hand how difficult it is to build a successful business and be home at the same time. My career requires that I spend a lot of time traveling and sleeping in hotel rooms. However, my family knows how much I love them, and that's the most important gift I can give them."

That brings to mind what the late great Jim Rohn used to say: 'For every promise, there's a price to pay.' In other words, if we want a particular result, we need to take the actions required to get that result."

"That's exactly what I want my sales staff to realize," Sherman said. "I want them to answer these questions: Have you ever seriously considered the cost? The price you must pay if you ever hope to become a great salesperson? What are you willing to give up, to get what you really want? Will you give up some golf, poker, softball, bridge, TV, or other diversions now, so you can create a dream lifestyle for your future?"

William chimed in. "This is what I've learned. There can be no progress, no achievement without sacrifice. Sales champions know they have to pay something in order to get what they want. Ordinary salespeople don't understand that. They are deluded by the thought of getting something for nothing. But all you get when you employ the 'something-for-nothing-rule-of-thinking' is nothing."

I nodded. "Success will not come to you automatically and easily. You have to pay the price if you want to get what you want. Part of paying the price is the willingness to do whatever it takes to get the job done."

"My father was a professional boxer; he taught me a lot of important lessons. One of the most meaningful lessons he taught me was, "'To be successful in business, you have to eat and breathe success.'" Until you get to that point, he said, "'It's unlikely you'll succeed.'"

Our drinks arrived and we paused a moment to enjoy the first sips.

Refreshed, I continued. "It took me two years to complete this book. Every day, new obstacles got in my way. There were moments where doubt and the fear of failure crept into my mind and tried to steal my dream.

"But I refused to quit or give up. Most mornings, I started writing at 4:30 a.m. before my regular workday began. Some nights I worked until midnight. It's been a grueling two-year journey, but I stayed on task and paid the price."

"I understand what you're saying," Jenna Gomez said. "To win at whatever it is you decide to do in life, you need to be willing to pay the price. Here is my personal mantra: I will pay the price to do today what others will not do, so tomorrow, I can do what others cannot do."

"But sacrifice isn't enough," I replied. "Otherwise you're spinning your wheels. I address that in Principle Thirty: Work Harder."

Key Lessons

- Every day, we have the option to live our lives with passion, be open to possibility, and reach for the stars. We have the freedom to boldly live, laugh, and love.

- If you want to reach your full potential, then you must face up to these three truths:
  1. You have more potential within you than you realize.
  2. You likely have settled for the life you now live.
  3. Once you unlock your mind from self-limiting thoughts, you can discover the talents and gifts you were given to live a happy life.

- God didn't create you to be average. You were created to excel. The big challenge of life is to become all that you have the potential of becoming.

- Often the only thing holding salespeople back from greater success is that they can't visualize themselves as being more successful. It may take years, but to experience excellence, you must first create a vision of excellence in your mind.

- If you want an extraordinary sales career, realize there is a price to pay. Part of paying the price is the willingness to do whatever it takes to get the job done.

Key Principle # 30

Work Harder

David McDonald spoke up. "I have a quote from Colin Powell. 'A dream doesn't become reality through magic; it takes sweat, determination and hard work.'"

"Good example," I noted. "If you think being a sales champion is easy, you're wrong. It can be fun, but it's not easy. It requires hard work. A sales champion does not arrive at the top of the mountain on day one."

Sherman explained, "Just because someone makes it look easy doesn't mean many long hours weren't invested. If becoming a great salesperson is important to you, then you need to make the effort."

Sherman pointed to the wall clock and said, "Success doesn't fall into the laps of clock watchers. It's earned by people who work until they meet their goals, not walk out the door at 5:00 o'clock."

I amplified Sherman's comment by saying, "There's a common belief that the salespeople who sell the most are 'gifted' and work very little. Yes, they may have better selling skills, but if you study these people, you learn that they work a lot more hours than the average salesperson.

"We are constantly bombarded with rags-to-riches stories and overnight successes. While that sells books and gets media attention, the reality for these high achievers is that they were willing to go the extra mile, which got them to the top.

"How many times have you heard that someone excels at something because he or she was 'born into it'? Great salespeople aren't born; they're made through an intense desire and willingness to keep going even when they feel like they have no more to give.

"Usually, we only acknowledge sales champions after they've achieved success. When we look at them, we see the results of their blood, sweat, and tears. We don't see the effort that built those results. And that's a shame because it leads to a skewed understanding of what led to their success."

"That brings to mind a study I'm familiar with," Jenna said. "In the 1990's the psychologist K. Anders Ericsson and two colleagues at Berlin's Academy of Music compared amateur pianists with professional pianists. The striking thing about the study is that he and his colleagues couldn't find any 'naturals,' that is, musicians who ascended to the top while practicing a fraction of the time their peers did."

"Which proves my point," I replied. "The notion that sales champions are born is a myth. There is no such thing as the natural-born salesperson any more than there is a natural-born physician, attorney, athlete, or pianist. People may naturally possess certain attributes such as charisma, humor, and likability. But these characteristics alone won't make one exceptional.

"British-based researchers Michael J. Howe, Jane W. Davidson, and John A. Sluboda concluded in another study that, 'The evidence we have surveyed does not support the notion that excelling is a consequence of possessing innate gifts.' For the first time in history, science was able to provide the evidence of what enlightened people have claimed throughout the ages."

Sherman chuckled. "Show me a salesperson you think has 'natural ability,' and I'll show you a person who has made a commitment to achieve his or her heart's desire over the long haul."

"Greatness is not mysterious," I said. "Behind every great person is a story of training, practice, discipline and sacrifice. Joe Louis, a world heavyweight boxing champion, said it best: 'A champion doesn't become a champion in the ring. He is merely recognized in the ring. The becoming happens during his daily routine.'"

"Hard work always trumps raw talent," William rejoined. "That's what average salespeople have to realize. Salespeople who focus on hard work will always move forward while talented salespeople who don't follow through with hard work will lose."

Successful salespeople work hard. Most people want to be successful but they aren't prepared to work hard to achieve it. Sales champions don't wait for business to come to them; they go after it. They usually start work earlier than their colleagues and stay later than everyone else. They make more telephone prospecting calls, set more qualified appointments, get more referrals, give more sales presentations and close more profitable sales than their colleagues.

I retrieved my wallet and pulled out an old newspaper clipping, which I unfolded. "Here's an article I've saved about Herb Brooks being enshrined into the Hockey Hall of Fame. Herb was the Olympic hockey coach whose team won the gold medal beating the Russians in 1980."

I passed the article across the table.

"The USA team was made up of kids in college and the Russians were professionals. For years, many sports writers called this win a miracle and voted it the best single sports victory of the 20th century.

"Dan Brooks, Herb's son, is quoted in the article as saying, 'He always told me, it really wasn't a miracle, it was hard work, 10 months of blood, sweat, and tears. Those 20 guys worked their tails off.'"

The article returned to me. I carefully folded and returned it to my wallet.

"Most successful salespeople, if compared to the average salesperson, work *extremely* hard. However, just because you're working harder than the *average salesperson* doesn't mean you're actually working hard.

"To determine whether you are working hard, you must compare yourself to some of the hardest working people on the planet.

"Here's a story about a family who worked about as hard as human beings can. I'm sure you've never heard of Yolanda and Rogelio Garcia Sr. I hadn't either until I stumbled across a story about how they had put their kids through college.

"Yolanda and her husband were undocumented immigrants from Mexico who came to this country for a better life. They became citizens and held jobs in factories and in kitchens. During all their years, even when work was slow, they have never collected a handout or a dime of welfare because there was always the trash."

"Trash?" Jenna asked.

"The Garcias supported their family by picking through trash, often cutting their fingers on broken glass while searching for cans and bottles. They make their living in the darkened streets and back alleys of Los Angeles, recycling other people's cans and bottles for cash. They collected more than 8 million cans and bottles to help put two children through college.

"Stories like this remind us that our 'hard work' probably isn't as hard as we think."

Strengthen Your Commitment

Sherman Jackson waited for me in the lobby of his company, Palisade Global Mutual. "The feedback I've been hearing is really positive," he said. "My sales staff has been energized by your presentation. We're looking forward to today's session."

He led me to the main training room. The salespeople were settling in, cups of coffee in hand, notebooks open and computers plugged in.

I took my place at the front of the room. Fresh markers were lined up on the trough below the white board, ready for use.

"Good morning," I said. "We'll begin today's session with a quote from a man we are all familiar with, Tony Robbins. He said, 'There's a difference between interest and commitment. When you're interested in doing something, you do it only when circumstances permit. When you're committed to something, you accept no excuse, only results.' Which leads us to Principle Thirty-one: Strengthen Your Commitment."

I wrote *Commitment* on the white board.

"Before we proceed, can someone give me the definition?"

David McDonald raised his hand. He read from his laptop. "The Merriam-Webster dictionary defines commitment as the state or an instance of being obligated or emotionally impelled."

I then asked, "What does that really mean?" David said, "It means you make a decision, and you stick to that decision, no matter how much it hurts, no matter what it costs, you stick to it."

Jenna added, "Commitment is persistence, being unstoppable in your pursuits. It is going that extra mile to get you where you want to go. It is the do or die attitude, the never give up mind set."

"All success begins with a thought, but what makes thoughts

become reality is commitment." Without effort, focus, and commitment, no forward steps are taken. Without commitment, it is difficult to reach your *full* potential in life."

A thought on its own can give you a temporary feeling of inspiration, but commitment is what gets you through the obstacles that life puts in front of you.

It is said that people don't know if they are committed until adversity strikes. I agree and said, "Commitment is most difficult and most readily proven during tough times. How someone weathers the storms of life most clearly demonstrates their personal commitment.

Life is like a voyage, and the circumstances of life are like the weather. Sometimes there is smooth sailing. But at other times we will encounter severe storms."

Maybe you didn't get the sale you already spent your commission check on. Perhaps you lost your job in the middle of a recession. Maybe you've experienced an accident, grave illness or other personal tragedy; this is when it is easiest to compromise your commitments.

A wise man once said, *"obstacles are things a person sees when he takes his eyes off the goal."* Another said, *"obstacles are opportunities in disguise."* Let's not view the challenges in our lives as hindrances, but rather view them as opportunities in disguise.

I locked eyes with the salespeople. "Many people pursue their goals based on their emotions, the way they feel. If they are feeling good they can follow through on their commitments. If they don't feel like it then they find a way to ignore their commitment.

But true commitment does not work like that. It is not dependent on how you feel. Feelings go up and down like a roller coaster, depending on what is going on in our lives, but true commitment is rock solid.

"Commitment is a matter of choice. It is a decision you make. Conditions should not determine your commitment, your passion should."

Top performing salespeople view success for themselves and others as largely a function of commitment and motivation, not luck, random chance or external factors.

"I hate to break the news to you, but becoming a great salesperson is not a 'stroll in the park.' It takes focus, 100 percent effort, and 'never say die' perseverance. You have to really commit to it. You have to believe in your heart you can do it and you deserve it. If you are not fully committed to being a great salesperson, chances are you won't be.

"When you commit to achieving a result that you care about, when you're 'in it with your heart,' things will come your way. Commitment, says James Womack, 'unlocks the doors of imagination, allows vision, and gives us the *right stuff* to turn our dreams into reality.'"

"If you study the success stories of great people, you will notice that they are 100 percent committed to their dreams and goals. They are willing to pour their hearts and souls into accomplishing what they want. This is what contributes to their greatness. On the other hand, ordinary people just talk and dream about what they want, but they are not really committed to make things happen."

Jenna Gomez spoke up. "Is commitment one big all-or-nothing choice?"

"No," I replied. "Commitment, as we've seen, is made up of many choices, often small, made many times over. As a matter of fact, when it comes to big goals, small commitments matter most."

I drew the Olympic logo on the white board. "Let's look at this example. A swimmer commits to achieving her best result at the Olympics. So each morning at 5:00 a.m., she commits to getting out of bed, and commits to the pool for training--even though she feels like sleeping in. And she does it over and over and over again, day after day--until she achieves her desired result. That's commitment!

"It is the steps that you take each and every day that are responsible for the results you will get. Success is not about getting big results or big achievement; it is about the commitment of taking one small step at a time. And eventually you will reach your goals and achieve your dreams."

Bill Gates talks about the 'spiral of success', on which you build upon your small successes, one on top of another, like he did with Microsoft. Soon, all those small victories add up into a spiral that continues to go up and up.

Sherman addressed the room. "Here's another great example of commitment. A young man once asked Socrates how he could acquire wisdom. Socrates told him, 'Come with me.' He took the young man to a river and shoved his head under water, holding it there until the young man struggled for air. Then Socrates lifted his head from the water and let him breathe.

"Once the young man had regained his composure, Socrates asked him, 'What did you desire most when your head was underwater and you couldn't breathe?' The man replied, 'I wanted air.' Socrates said, 'When your desire for wisdom is as passionate as your desire to breathe, then you will find wisdom.'"

I turned to the class. "How badly do you want to be a great salesperson? If you desire greatness as badly as that young man wanted air, then greatness will arrive. But if you don't have that burning desire and unwavering commitment, then you won't become a great salesperson.

"The benefits of commitment are not just what commitment does for you, but what it does inside you."

I erased the white board to prepare for the next topic. "Now we move on to Principle Thirty-two: Stretch to the Next Level."

Key Principle # 32

Stretch to the Next level

I wrote on the board *Comfort Zone*. "What do we mean by this term?"

William Daniels answered: "Comfort Zone describes a type of mental conditioning that creates artificial mental boundaries that offer a false sense of security. The comfort zone is a person's internal and external areas of control."

"Correct," I noted. "The challenge is to move out of your comfort zone. Brian Tracy said, 'You can only grow if you are willing to feel awkward and uncomfortable when you try something new.'

"Your comfort zone is a collection of internal and external conditions you have grown accustomed to. Although settling into your comfort zone may be tempting, there are times when your comfort zone turns into a self-constructed trap, keeping you from realizing your full potential."

"Over time, we all gather a set of constricting habits and routines around us—ones that trap us in a zone of supposed comfort, well below what our potential would allow us to attain.

"I often talk about the routines we get stuck in. Here's an example. Many people wake up on Monday, wash their face, brush their teeth, get something to eat, drive to work, get some work done, have lunch, drive home, have dinner, watch some TV, put the kids to bed, fall asleep and do the same things all over again on Tuesday, Wednesday, Thursday, and Friday."

The salespeople followed the cadence of my illustration with knowing smiles.

"Pretty soon, such daily routines slip below the level of our consciousness and end up setting the standards as to what we think *we can* and *cannot do*."

I drew a carnival tent on the board. "Let me share with you the story about a young boy who went to a carnival. He saw a sign that said, 'See a live elephant for only 15 cents.' He bought a ticket and entered a tent where a large, docile elephant was standing. The boy was amazed because the elephant appeared unrestrained. When he took a closer look, he noticed a thin rope tying the elephant's right foot to a skinny pole in the center of the tent. The curious boy asked the elephant trainer, 'How can that little rope hold an elephant? He looks like he could easily pull free if he wanted to.'

"The elephant trainer replied, 'He could but he doesn't know it. When the elephant was very young, we had him chained to a thick stake. The elephant would tug at it all day long but discovered no matter how hard he pulled, the chain would not work loose. After he stopped tugging, we replaced the chain with a thin rope. Now that the elephant is big and strong, he's stopped trying to break the rope because he thinks he can't.'"

I sketched a picture of a thin rope on the board and under it wrote the word *Thought*. "Is there a self-limiting thought (I pointed to the thin rope on the white board), holding you back from your goals and dreams? If so, it's time to break free and expose the greatness that's inside you."

Think for a moment about the most significant accomplishments you've attained professionally or personally, your own personal best. Perhaps it was a record sales month, winning a major contest, coaching a winning team, or running a marathon.

I don't know you or your circumstances, but my bet is that you did not attain your personal best while you kept doing the same things. My guess is you achieved your personal best when you attacked the status quo, not when you comfortably sat in your rocking chair wrapped-up in your comfort zone. The most significant accomplishments we rack up in our lives are when we step out of our comfort zone, not when we sit still.

I drew a net around the words *Comfort Zone*. "You feel safe in your comfort zone. And I understand it's difficult to exit your comfort zone, but that is the only way to free yourself from your self-imposed prison and live a more exciting life."

I sketched a stick figure of a salesperson and scribbled a line below it. "Too many salespeople live below their potential. They have special gifts and talents. But they're comfortable and satisfied where they are."

"Humans are wired to seek comfort, and as a result, much of their daily life is focused around familiar patterns and habits. When something threatens to break those habits, we feel uncomfortable and nervous.

Realise it can be exciting and rewarding to get out of your comfort zone despite what your thoughts and feelings might be telling you before you get started.

"If you want to become a sales champion, you must step out of your comfort zone and reach new heights." I drew a dinosaur above the stick figure. "Otherwise, you'll end up like the dinosaur – extinct."

Motivational speaker and author Jim Rohn said, "Any day we wish, we can discipline ourselves to change. Any day we wish, we can open the book that will open our mind to new knowledge. Any day we wish, we can start a new activity. Any day we wish, we can start the process of life change. We can do it immediately, or next week, or next month, or next year."

He went on to say, "We can also do nothing. We can pretend rather than perform. And if the idea of having to change ourselves makes us uncomfortable, we can remain as we are. We can choose rest over labor, entertainment over education, delusion over truth, and doubt over confidence. The choices are ours to make. But while we curse the effect, we continue to nourish the cause."

It's time to pin down unhealthy thinking patterns and daily routines that are unconsciously running your life and get rid of them.

Here's how to do it:

1. Understand the truth about your thinking and daily routines.
2. Interpret your thoughts differently. No new thoughts, no learning. No learning, no access to successful change.
3. Choose to do something that's out of character for you. Do something different and see what happens.
4. Make new acquaintances. If you do the same things with the same people in the same ways, you'll keep getting the same results. Do something different with a new group of people.
5. Face your own truth.

I moved to a new panel of the white board and wrote, *Risk*.

"Author and motivational speaker Leo Buscaglia said, 'The person who risks nothing, does nothing, has nothing, is nothing, and becomes nothing. He may avoid suffering and sorrow, but he simply cannot learn and feel and change and grow and love and live.'

"He was talking about Principle Thirty-three: Take More Risks."

Key Lessons

- Success doesn't fall into the laps of clock watchers. It's earned by people who work until they meet their goals, not walk out the door at 5:00 o'clock.

- Great salespeople aren't born; they're made through an intense desire and willingness to keep going when they fee like they have no more to give.

- Hard work always trumps raw talent. Salespeople who focus on hard work will always move forward while talented salespeople who don't follow through with hard work will lose.

- There's a difference between interest and commitment. When you're interested in doing something, you do it only when circumstances permit. When you're committed to something, you accept no excuses, only results.

- Committed salespeople do not get sidetracked easily; they stay the course even when there is great inconvenience or adversity.

- Although settling into your comfort zone may be tempting, there are times when your comfort zone turns into a self-constructed trap, keeping you from realizing your full potential.

- It can be fun and rewarding to get out of your comfort zone despite what your mind and feelings might be telling you before you get started.

Key Principle # 33

Take More Risks

Taking risks means daring to try new ideas with no predictable control over the results or consequences. Risk taking requires a willingness to make mistakes and tackle challenging situations without obvious solutions.

To achieve your goals and dreams, you have to take responsible risks. If you do, maybe you'll achieve your dreams or maybe you won't. But if you never take the risk, you'll never know.

"Most people don't like taking risks." I pointed to the white board where earlier I had written *Comfort Zone* with a safety net around it. "They would much rather stay where they're at than risk losing something they already have. So when it comes to risking what we have for what we *could* have, it's difficult to get people motivated to act.

"Can anyone give me two examples of risk?"

Jenna said, "Physical risk. The chance of injury or getting killed."

"Which I'm not advocating," I replied, to laughter.

"Social risk," David commented. "The likelihood of feeling embarrassment, shame, guilt, or the loss of affection or respect from others."

"Which I describe as the 'bruised-ego syndrome.'

"Of all the things a salesperson should fear, being unable to take risks should head the list. The only real risk in sales is playing it safe, following the same boring routine day in and day out. The minute you decide not to take a risk is when your competitors will pass you by."

Sales champions must be risk-takers. Fact is, sales champions take calculated risks and accept them as part of the journey to greater success. By contrast, ordinary salespeople settle into their comfort zones and stop challenging themselves. They are unwilling to take risks in order to achieve their dreams.

"Having written a book called *The Secret to Sales Greatness* and often speaking to sales professionals, I'm regularly asked by ambitious salespeople what risks I suggest they take. **Here are my top five suggestions for any sales professional:**"

1. Stand up for what you believe.
2. Say what you feel. But say it in a nurturing tone of voice.
3. Face the truth.
4. Regularly step outside your comfort zone.
5. Be assertive (not pushy) rather than passive.

"Many of the risks salespeople face are rather small. There's not much to lose and a lot to gain. Nevertheless, ordinary salespeople struggle with risk because they're unable to exit from their comfort zone. Salespeople who are unwilling or unable to take risks will become ineffective, if not obsolete."

"Have you ever noticed that most successful people have one thing in common. Nine times out of ten there was some degree of risk involved in their success. Successful people believe that success and risk go hand and hand."

There's always a certain amount of risk involved no matter what we do. But isn't it better to take the risk. Or is it better to look back at the end of your career and life and say, "I wish I'd taken that risk?"

Sherman added, "In a study conducted by Cornell University, senior citizens were asked about their life's regrets. The overwhelming response was that most regretted not doing what they had always wanted to do. It was the risks they didn't take--not the setbacks that happened--that haunted them the most."

"The risk of staying stagnant is much worse than the risk of exploring opportunity, even though it's scary."

"For example," I said, "the story of English entrepreneur Richard Branson reads like a financial fairy tale. A middle-class English lad without the benefit of a high school education started his first business at the age of 18--a newspaper targeting students--and made his first million by 23. By 1992, he was worth a cool billion. Though known as a daredevil, Branson has a practical philosophy of risk. 'Before starting any new venture, I consider the downside,' he says. 'I ask myself, can I afford the worst that could happen?'

"To perform at a higher level, you have to step out of your comfort zone and do things differently. There has to come a point when you say, "I'm really comfortable where I'm at. I sleep really well. Now, I need to go in another direction and challenge myself."

You need to challenge yourself if you want to propel your success to that next level, because sales is not an environment where safety and success work well together. To be successful in sales, you need to get comfortable being uncomfortable.

"In sales, you can't be successful by walking the safe road just for the sake of safety. Sales champions go where there is no path and create their own trail." T.S. Eliot said, "Only those who will risk going too far can possibly find out how far one can go."

I drew a stick figure on a tight-rope. "Sales champions 'work on the edge' and take risks.

"Papa Wallenda, the great wire walker said, 'Life is lived out on the wire. The rest is just waiting.'"

I began the next session with Principle Thirty-four: Be a Balanced Thinker.

Key Principle # 34

Be a Balanced Thinker

The major problem in sales is not really a problem with sales. It's a thinking problem.

We are moving away from a society of salespeople with logical and linear abilities to a society of salespeople built of balanced thinkers.

Balanced thinking means utilizing your right-brain and left-brain thinking. To help everyone understand the concept of right-brain and left-brain thinking. I drew on the white board a picture of the human brain with its two hemispheres.

"This theory suggests that the two different sides of the brain control two different 'modes' of thinking. It also suggests that each of us prefers one mode over the other."

This concept was developed from the research in the late 1960's by the American psycho-biologist Roger W. Sperry. He discovered the human brain has two very different ways of thinking: Right-brain and left-brain.

William Daniels asked, "Are we then totally left-brained or totally right-brained?"

I replied, "No one is totally left-brained or totally right-brained. Just as you have a dominant hand and a dominant eye, you have a dominant side of your brain."

"We tend to process information using our dominant side. However, the thinking and communication process is enhanced when both sides of the brain function in a balanced manner.

"The most successful salespeople I know are "balanced thinkers." That is to say they have no predominance, so they can think logically and methodically but, equally, they can be creative and not confined by specific thinking paradigms."

I drew a circle around the entire brain.

David McDonald raised his hand. "How are the right-brain/left brain concepts relevant to sales?"

I gestured to the board and said, "Sales is the cross-roads where both right and left brain thinking meet."

Here were two examples. "When you prepare for a sales presentation, you should be able to visualize the end result in your mind, then sit down and map out the details of the presentation. That involves the right brain, which works on various things simultaneously.

"But at the same time, you must be able to look critically at what you're planning to present, what questions you'll ask, how you'll build rapport, what benefits you'll offer, and what next steps you'll agree on. That's the left brain, being analytical.

"After finding out whether your thinking is dominated by your right or left brain, you then can deliberately set out to use 'balanced thinking' during your presentation. Balanced thinking means using both sides of your brain - both of which are part of our everyday life."

By using "'balanced thinking'" you will be surprised by what new results you can produce.

Here was the second example.

"To be successful at selling, you must know your brain dominance, and that of your prospects and customers, so you can establish rapport, adapt your message, and bridge the communication gap that often exists between buyers and sellers."

Sherman spoke up, "Without rapport and effective communication there is no sale."

"That's a fact," I replied. "People do business with people who think and act like they do.

"Looking at how the brain processes information will help us better understand the preferences, attitudes, and behaviors of consumers – what they're really thinking. The more we can understand our customers' thinking patterns, the more likely we are to establish rapport and meet their buying motives. And when that happens, we all win."

I divided the white board with a vertical line. To the left of the line, I wrote: Left Brain. To the right: Right Brain.

Under Left Brain, I wrote: You focus on words, symbols, and numbers. You remember names rather than faces. All this means you are verbal.

Under Right Brain, I jotted: You focus on images and patterns. You take "mental photos" to remember things. You are primarily visual.

"How do you process that information into ideas? For a left-brain person, you process ideas sequentially. You work up to the whole step-by-step, focusing on details, and keeping information highly organized. You learn by observing." I jotted those concepts on the board.

"Now for right-brain. You process ideas simultaneously. You see the whole first, then the details. You learn by absorbing sensory input, touching and feeling the actual objects."

I paused a moment to let the class catch up with their notes.

"Back to left brain. You are analytical, and you make logical deductions from information. You like to make to-do lists.

"Now to the right brain. You are intuitive, meaning you are led by feelings. You can make lateral connections from information."

I listed the concepts under the appropriate headings.

"Again to the Left Brain. You like to plan ahead and are good at tracking time.

"Right Brain. You have no sense of time and have trouble prioritizing, so you're often late and impulsive."

Jenna Gomez asked, "I like to know why I'm supposed to do something or why the rules even exist. I also find myself listening to the 'how' something is said rather than the 'what.' Does that make me right or left-brained?"

Right-brain for sure," I answered. "A left-brain person is likely to follow rules without questioning them, and listen to 'what' is being said."

David motioned that he wanted to contribute. He said, "I'm one of those guys who will spend hours with an instruction manual. I can also memorize spelling and math formulas very easily. Which side of the brain do I use?"

"Left brain for sure," I answered. "A right-brain person is unlikely to read an instruction manual and has trouble finding words to express himself or herself." I asked, "Do you talk with your hands?"

"No," he replied, smiling.

"Left brain behavior," I noted. "Right brain people talk with their hands."

I stepped back from the board to review what I'd written.

I turned around to face my audience. "Here's the bottom line: "The reality is that many salespeople never reach their maximum potential because they don't capitalize on the different skills of each side of the brain. Salespeople need to be organized, disciplined, analytical strategists, but they also need to be creative visionaries who are unafraid to constantly challenge paradigms.

"We do not need predominantly left-brained or predominantly right-brained salespeople. We need salespeople to strengthen both sides, thus bringing themselves into perfect alignment with their prospects and customers."

It's easy to fall into a rut with our thinking because, although the brain is a very powerful organ, it is extremely lazy. It's easy to become a couch potato doing the same type of thinking over and over again, and never exercise the maximum potential of the mind.

I used a marker to circle the picture I had drawn of the brain. "As you stretch and flex your brain to bring it into balance, it is important to not look from which side is the better side, but rather that each side of the brain is valuable. It is the blending of 'balanced thinking' that leads salespeople to greater success and a competitive edge in the marketplace."

This principle served as the foundation for the next session, Principle Thirty-five: You Can't Manage Time.

Key Principle # 35

You Can't Manage Time

During the past 25 years, there have been hundreds of books written about time management. I cautioned the audience and said, "Stop wasting your time trying to manage time. No matter how hard you try, you can't manage time."

The salespeople in the classroom gave me a collective expression which seemed to say, *Can't manage time?* It was an idea bordering on the ridiculous for people in our business.

I explained, "We're all familiar with the well-worn phrase, 'Time is money,' and the need for each of us to manage our time. So what do I mean, 'You can't manage time?'

"Let's return to, 'Time is Money.' The difference between the two is that money can be recouped but time cannot. Time is elusive, intangible, and finite. Time is your most precious resource."

Sherman Jackson turned to the group. "Let me illustrate that with this analogy. Imagine a benefactor depositing $86,400 into your checking account every day, for you to invest as you choose. Imagine what you could do with this gift. Did you ever realize that every day, you receive a gift of 86,400 seconds of time? How you use that gift is up to you."

I continued. "Your success and your overall sense of personal satisfaction depend on your ability to master the skill of time management. Of course, in reality, you can't manage time. The clock ticks off the seconds, minutes, and hours while you do what you do or don't do. Time management is self-management. It's managing yourself in relation to time."

Time is the only common denominator that sales champions and ordinary salespeople share.

"Time is distributed equally. How much time do we each have?"

David McDonald answered, "60 seconds in a minute."

Jenna Gomez said, "60 minutes in an hour."

William Daniels added, "24 hours in a day."

Roger Unger said, "168 hours in a week."

I explained, "We start each day with the same 24 hours. Once it's gone, you cannot get it back. Therefore, time is much more precious than money.

"Time is both a wonderful and terrible thing. No one has enough time to do everything he or she would like to do, yet everyone has all the time there is. You may be certain that you need more time, but you're not going to get it. This leaves you with two options: Either learn to sleep faster..."

The room laughed.

"...or learn to invest your time better."

The mistake many salespeople make is to say yes to too many things, so that they live according to the priorities of others rather than according to their own. They fail to recognize that doing one thing means that they are not doing something else. Every time you agree to do any one thing, something else you might have done will not get done.

Are you a doormat when it comes to allowing prospects and customers to control your time? Do they walk all over it? Is your calendar an open invitation for them to waste your time? When this happens, their inefficiency becomes your inefficiency. Their wasted time becomes your wasted time.

"You have the right to invest your own time on your 'high-pay' sales activities. You have the ability to say no to others. No to time-wasting meetings. No to new meaningless obligations. No to taking on the work of others.

"One of the distinguishing characteristics of most top performing salespeople is they get things done by defending their time. They eliminate and avoid activities that would distract them from accomplishing their goals. As a result, they have time for the important things in their lives."

Have you noticed that top performing salespeople always seem to have time - they make time - for the important things in their lives.

"Your answers to these three questions will make you more aware of how you use your time."

I wrote on the board and said,

"1. What's the best use of my time right now?"

I again wrote and said,

"2. Is what I'm doing getting me closer to or further away from my goals?"

And finally:

"3. Am I doing what's easiest, or am I doing what's best?"

I faced the audience. "Do you think and behave as if your sales career is a practice session, with the 'big game' coming down the road? Only after the years have slipped away do many salespeople realize they were playing in the 'big game' every day. Treat every minute of every day as the 'big game' because every minute of every day counts!"

I moved to the next panel of white board. "Now to Principle Thirty-six: Do What You Don't Like Doing."

Key Lessons

- To achieve your goals and dreams, you have to take responsible risks.

- Salespeople who are unwilling or unable to take risks will become ineffective, if not obsolete.

- The most successful salespeople are 'balanced thinkers.'

- That is to say they have no predominance, so they can think logically and methodically, but equally, they can be creative and not be confined by specific thinking paradigms.

- People do business with people that think and act like they do.

- No matter how hard you try, you can't manage time.

- Time management is self-management. It's managing yourself in relation to time.

- Top performing salespeople defend their time. They eliminate and avoid activities that would distract them from accomplishing their daily goals.

Key Principle # 36

Do What You Don't Like Doing

Do you want to be a great salesperson? No problem! Just do the sales behaviors you don't feel like doing. That's how to inch your way to greater success. Of course, that's easier said than done because we have trained ourselves to do only what we feel like doing.

What are the most important sales behaviors you should be doing every day? Are you doing those behaviors first?

"Think about what behaviors you perform throughout the day, and which ones contribute the most to your success. What you'll discover is that your days are consumed with low-pay activities that really don't contribute much to your overall success.

"Let me quote Peter Drucker, a writer, management consultant, and university professor who made an important contribution to business when he differentiated between the words efficiency and effectiveness. Drucker said, 'Efficiency is doing things right. Effectiveness is doing the right things.'"

Sherman Jackson commented, "To get on the 'fast track' of success, determine the sales activities--*the right things*--that are most important for achieving your goals and do those activities first."

I announced to the room, "Are you spending a lot of time working on urgent things, but not on important things? How much of your time do you invest on urgent tasks that require immediate attention versus the important ones that will actually help you reach your goals?"

Urgent things are not always important and important things are not always urgent. If you get bogged down with urgent tasks that aren't important instead of working on your important sales tasks, you're building your sales career on a slippery-slope and it's only a matter of time before your goals slip away.

Since there is always more work than time, setting priorities will help you manage your daily activities. The secret to prioritizing your work for maximum results isn't that everything gets done, but that the activities most important for the achievement of your goals, get done.

Little things done well can make a big difference. To transform yourself from an average sales rep into a sales champion, invest time during your *money hours*, 6:30 a.m. to 6:30 p.m. working on your 'high-pay' sales tasks."

I readied a marker. **"What are high-pay sales tasks?"**

The salespeople shouted answers, and I jotted them on the board.

"Prospecting."

"Cold calling."

"Asking for referrals and introductions."

"Closing sales."

"Qualifying prospects."

"Presenting to decision-makers."

"New appointments."

"Following up."

"Generating leads."

"Customer service work."

A comprehensive list. I nodded in approval and said, "According to a recent Selling Skills Institute study, sales reps invest on average only three percent of their time actually selling. Low-pay and no-pay tasks, such as paperwork, administrative duties, travel, and other activities, consume the majority of their 'money hours.'"

I drew a large circle on the board and divided it into a pie chart as I explained, "The results of the study show sales activity as a percent of time:

"Face-to-face selling, three percent.

"Prospecting, three percent.

"Servicing customers, twenty-six percent.

"Problem solving, twenty-five percent.

"Sales meetings, four percent.

"Travel time, fifteen percent.

"Administrative work, twenty-four percent.

I pointed to the chart. "As you can see, only a few hours in each day are actually devoted to working on high-pay sales activities. High-pay sales activities are the daily activities that help get you closer to your goals. They're the behaviors that really matter"

I wrote the word goals next to the chart and an arrow from the chart to the word goals. "Are you working on activities that move you closer to or further away from your goals?"

It was time to segue into Principle Thirty-seven: Be a Lifelong Learner.

Be a Lifetime Learner

Sherman Jackson, his Vice-President of Sales Roger Unger, and their sales staff were in the classroom, ready for the next session.

I began, "In Western society, we often think of 'learning' in very narrow terms: it's what we do in school, and once we've got our college degree, the learning phase is over – it's time to work.

"Sales champions are never on vacation from their favorite pastime: the commitment to never-ending learning. Learning doesn't end when the school bell rings. It's a lifelong endeavor, but too many salespeople come to the mistaken conclusion that when school is over, they are done learning. If you want to be a sales champion--and if you're in this class, I hope that you are--the learning process must never end."

I quoted Hugh Nibley, a scholar and university professor, who had said, "Our search for knowledge should be ceaseless...never resting on laurels, degrees or past achievements."

"Always make sure your mind is open to new information; never be so closed-minded that you're not learning something new every day. If you take the time to consciously learn new things, you'll find that life is more rewarding."

Sherman commented, "Highly successful people are lifetime learners. They are never satisfied with what they already know."

Philosopher John Dewey said it quite well: 'Education is not preparation for life; education is life itself.'"

"So true," I added. "Highly successful people have a continual thirst for knowledge and are always looking to learn and grow."

It's hard to get to a more senior position in the world of golf officiating than Clyde Luther. At 81, the former United Airlines pilot from Burke, Va., has worked at more than 115 USGA championships, beginning with the U.S. Junior Amateur in 1982. "Education and on-course experience are the keys to being a good Rules official," says Luther, who estimates that he has attended more than 50 USGA/PGA of America Rules of Golf workshops as either a student or instructor. "There is always something new to learn."

You may be thinking, with everything that's going on, who has time for learning?

With today's technology, you can learn anywhere. You can learn at home, in school, at the office, or in your car.

Motivational speaking legend Zig Ziglar coined the term "Automobile University" to describe using time spent in one's vehicle on such worthwhile endeavors as listening to personal and professional development materials. The idea being that the same amount of time that is normally spent listening to music, that while it may be enjoyable isn't going to necessarily help us improve or experience the benefits of personal growth (nor move us any closer to achieving the goals we've set for ourselves).

Instead, Mr. Ziglar suggested that we could be investing that time, which might otherwise be wasted -- listening to personal and professional audio programs that will increase our expertise in whatever particular topic we might choose.

Sherman said, "Never let it be said that all that can be known about the 'art' of selling has already been considered. There is always the opportunity for new discoveries and important new findings."

I continued, "What was good enough to get you where you are today will not be sufficient to get you to where you'll need to be in the future. Make the commitment to be better tomorrow than you were today in everything you do.

"If you settle back and decide that you've learned everything you need to know about sales, building relationships, and about succeeding in your career ... you'll lose out to competitors who are committed to continuous learning."

Ask yourself this question: "What have you done in the last day, week, month, or year to become your best?"

I readied my marker at the white board to write as I asked: "How many books have you read on professional salesmanship in the last month?

"How many sales or personal development CD's have you listened to?

"How many sales seminars have you attended during the past 12 months?

"What percentage of your income have you allocated to self-improvement and improving your craft of selling?"

"One of the longest-lasting investments you can make, with the best returns over time, is in yourself and in your craft. Investing in yourself and in your craft will help you improve your earning power, as well as provide you with a sense of fulfillment.

"If you're not investing in your personal development, rest assured, you will pay a price. In this volatile economy, the consequence for not learning and growing can be career ending."

Sherman elaborated. "Once a month, ask yourself. What can you start doing, stop doing, or change about what you are doing? Ask this question at the end of every selling day, 'How can I do better tomorrow?'"

I expanded on his comments. "Average salespeople aren't motivated to become better. They do what it takes to muddle through life, never searching for new methods, and never thinking about self-improvement. Their sales careers are like flat champagne, no fizz at all."

Here are some tips to gradually but firmly establish the habit of lifelong learning:

Always have a book

It doesn't matter if it takes you a year or a week to read a book. Always strive to have a book that you are reading, and take it with you so you can read it when you have time.

We all have to-do lists. These are the tasks we need to accomplish. Try to also have a "to-learn" list. On it you can write ideas for new areas of study. Maybe you would like to learn a new language, play an instrument, or improve your interpersonal skills. Whatever motivates you, write it down.

Get More Intellectual Friends

Investing more time with people who actually invest much of their time in learning new skills. Their habits will rub off on you.

Make it a Priority

Few external forces are going to persuade you to learn. The desire has to come from within.

Once you decide you want to make lifelong learning a habit, it is up to you to make it a priority in your life.

Key Principle # 38

Don't Be a Know-It-All

I stepped to the next section of the board. "Let's now discuss Principle Thirty-eight: Don't Be a Know-It-All."

The topic elicited smiles from the audience.

"We've all run into this person," I said. "He swoops in on an unsuspecting prospect, dominates all discussions, and gets more attention than Brad Pitt on the red carpet. This is the plight of Mr. Know-It-All, the person whose sole purpose in life is to remind everyone how smart he is."

I wrote *Know-It-All* on the board, then circled the words in red.

The know-it-all is a person who insists he or she knows everything and is always right.

"If you are going to be successful, you have to give up the *Know-It-All* attitude." I slashed through the circle with the red marker. "Salespeople who suffer from 'know-it-all thinking' refuse to acknowledge that good thinking and taking the appropriate action is the difference between performing as an average salesperson and an extraordinary salesperson."

David McDonald spoke up. "What about this example? Have you ever had a conversation where the person you are talking with contradicts everything you say? You make a point and they immediately take an opposing position or feel they need to up-stage you with a more impressive story."

William Daniels added, "A lot of salespeople have difficulty in considering alternative points of view. They look at only one element of a situation and exclude everything else. Their way to solve a problem seems to be the only way. They approach life from a self-centered point of view. *My way or the highway.*"

I replied, "Successful salespeople consider alternative points of view and deal with several sources of information. Their minds are open to new thinking based on additional information, opinions, data or reasoning, which may contradict their beliefs."

A mentor of mine shared this advice with me when I first started in the sales training business. "Assume you know nothing at all and learn something new through each situation you are exposed to. Don't act like you know everything - be humble. Humility allows a successful person to become intentionally modest which gives you an edge in the end, over those who think they know everything."

Roger Unger recited, "Being a learner and not a know-it-all is among the top grounding principles of most successful people. As a know-it-all you eventually get stuck with what you know, whereas being a learner, one is willing to be influenced by new information, opinions, or perspectives."

Here's the difference between the know-it-all salesperson and the learner. The know-it-alls:

• Sees their truth as the only truth; *learners* are open to others' viewpoints.

• Base their self-worth on being right; *learners* base theirs on what they give back.

• Can't be wrong, so if they make a mistake they find someone or something else to blame; *learners* can make mistakes, admit they don't have all the answers, and continue to be part of the solution.

• Find it difficult to adapt to change, and become weaker, less effective, and less influential over time; *learners* are curious and more readily adapt.

Former longshoreman and writer Eric Hoffer said: "In times of change, learners inherit the Earth, while the learned find themselves beautifully equipped to deal with a world that no longer exists."

I said, "Salespeople who are ruled by their egos tend to be filled with..."

I wrote and recited, "Conflict.

"Anxiety.

"Negativity.

"Disappointment.

"High stress levels."

While knowledge and self-confidence are good, having the "big head" is egotistical and only flattering to oneself. Nobody likes to be around "mister know-it-all."

I turned from the board. "Know-it-all salespeople are extraordinarily self-absorbed; they annoy prospects, customers, their bosses, and people around them. Unfortunately, very few buyers ever decide to work with them because they're only thinking of themselves. Only a tiny sliver of their thinking is devoted to the needs of prospects and customers. Empathy is the rare occasion where these salespeople think through the perspective of another person."

Roger noted, "People who act important are usually weak deep down inside. Their self-important attitude is a facade, intended to prevent you from seeing their weaknesses and to trick you into believing they're confident."

The reality is that most salespeople who brag about their own exploits or look for special attention are simply trying to build themselves up in the eyes of others--and that's because they don't perceive themselves as worthy of respect.

I remember talking to a client from California; she shared a story with me about her favorite actor, Leo DiCaprio. She said, "Whenever I see him around Los Angeles, he's always the low-key guy, usually with a baseball cap pulled down almost covering his eyes. He seems like an ordinary guy. One of the few giants in Hollywood who keeps it real and lets his life's passion and charitable work speak for him."

I explained, "Self-centered salespeople are the tragic heroes of selling who are trapped in their own delusional thought bubble. They hold on to misguided beliefs and irrational thoughts that contradict factual data. They judge the world from a narrow, self-serving perspective and maintain beliefs that are unrelated to reality.

"There is a great scene in the movie *Fiddler on the Roof* where Tevye listens to two men who are arguing. The first makes his case, and Tevye says, 'You're right.' The second man then makes his case, and Tevye once again says, 'You're right.'

"A third man insists, 'They can't both be right!' To which Tevye replies, 'You are also right.'"

Laughter rippled across the room.

I continued, "Several years ago, I had a chance to hear Tom Kelly speak, CEO of DEO, the world's foremost innovation company. I'll never forget something he said..."

I wrote on the white board: "Have strong opinions, but hold onto them lightly."

I faced the audience and added the punch line. "Because you just might be wrong."

Everyone makes mistakes from time to time, and a dignified awareness of one's own imperfections can attract more long-term admiration than simply being right all the time.

One of the key attributes of sales champions is their ability to admit, "I *might be wrong.*"

"I remember hearing a story about two salespeople sitting on opposite sides of a large conference table. In the middle of the table was a piece of bright yellow paper with a large red number, which appeared as a *9* to one salesperson, but as a *6* to the other." I wrote a *9* next to a *6*.

"If the first salesperson said, 'That's a nine,' we wouldn't be surprised to hear the second salesperson, who was sitting on the opposite side of the table say, "You're crazy! That's not a nine. Anyone can plainly see it's a six. What's wrong with you? That's a nine if I've ever seen one.'

"And so it goes, around and around, two salespeople stubbornly refusing to see things from the other person's point of view. If it is true that there is always more than one way of seeing things, then the challenge is to find other points of view and choose between them.

"The salesperson who thinks he knows everything is condemned to repeat what he's done in the past."

Sherman said, "We all need to face our uncomfortable truths. We can't simply sweep the truth under the rug in an attempt to make it go away. If we want to become top-performing salespeople, one of the first steps is to face the truth about ourselves. When there is a discrepancy between a belief and a fact, we are always better off acting on the fact rather than on the belief."

I noted, "The skill of looking for other perspectives lies in asking yourself some key questions."

I wrote, "What other points of view are there?

"How would someone else think about this?

"How else could I think about it?

"Could I be making a mistake in the way I am thinking?'

I paced in front of the room. "To address that, we moved on to Principle Thirty-nine: Have Passion - It's Paramount."

Key Principle # 39

Have Passion - It's Paramount

The next session began when I wrote on the white board, Principle Thirty-nine: Have Passion - It's Paramount.

I said, "Throughout history, a handful of people have achieved success beyond the ordinary, and each of these greats had a passionate love for the product he or she sold."

"People like Michael Dell who had a passion for selling computers and competing with IBM which led to the formation of Dell Corporation while he was only 19. Bill Gates who left Harvard midway through his studies to follow his heart's desire. Henry Ford's father wanted his son to follow his footsteps and become a farmer. Henry's heart was with the motor engine. After furious fights with his father, he left to chart his own course to create history by starting the Ford Motor Company."

Sherman Jackson took my statement as his cue to add, "This is a key point. It's important to enjoy what you're doing and believe in what you're selling. If you're selling half-heartedly, no amount of training or positive thinking can help you become a top performer."

I elaborated, "Being passionate about the products and services you sell makes the difference between making a few sales and having a phenomenal sales career. Passion is what fuels the engine that propels you toward your goals and dreams.

If you ask successful people what really helped them get where they are in life, invariably they'll talk about their special passion."

Martha Graham, an American dancer and choreographer, said: "Great dancers are not great because of their technique; they are great because of their passion.'"

I wrote *Passion* on the board. "What's your passion? What energizes you? What puts excitement in your voice? A sparkle in your eye? Is it your work, hobby, volunteering or some other source?"

I asked the salespeople, "What are you passionate about?"

A woman in the front row said, "I am passionate about exercising."

Jim Phillips said, I'm passionate about painting. I take an evening class once a week and try to find time each weekend to paint."

Someone else said, "I am passionate about my motorcycle and the freedom it gives me on the road."

Another offered, "I am an avid skier and I like to spend vacations on the ski slopes."

I could not forget Jenna. She said, "I am passionate about music and teaching."

"Great examples," I acknowledged.

"Successful people look forward to doing whatever it is that they're doing. While they look forward to weekends or vacations away, they aren't the ones getting heartburn on Sunday, dreading Monday morning. They have passion for life and their work, and if they find themselves doing something they dread, they won't do it for long."

Apple founder, Steve Jobs said in his Stanford Commencement address the following: "When I was 17, I read a quote that went something like: "If you live each day as if it was your last, someday you'll most certainly be right." It made an impression on me, and since then, for the past 33 years, I have looked in the mirror every morning and asked myself: "If today were the last day of my life, would I want to do what I am about to do today?" And whenever the answer has been "No" for too many days in a row, I know I need to change something."

"Do you enjoy your work? To be truly happy you have to be doing something you not only enjoy, but that helps you live the kind of life you want for yourself and your family."

Roger Unger addressed the audience, "Life should not a collection of days you manage to simply get through but of precious moments that keep the flame of passion burning. You can't do without passion because passion and life go hand-in-hand. It is passion that ultimately determines the extent to which you live your life."

"I personally don't see myself having any other options than following my passion. Without doing what I truly enjoy, life would be without meaning."

Roger continued. "I believe the poorest salesperson in the world is not the salesperson who doesn't have any clients. The poorest salesperson in the world is the salesperson who doesn't have passion."

I asked, "How closely is your current life aligned with your passions? Does your sales career inspire and motivate you to do more, be more, and accomplish more?" I pointed to the word Passion. "Because very few things are as infectious as a salesperson with passion. While work can sustain your daily living requirements, being passionate about your work is the fastest way to spur yourself to the top."

I leaned against the lectern. "I was surprised when Sherman Jackson asked me, 'What are you passionate about?' The question caught me off guard. Sometimes it's difficult to identify the things, beliefs and ideas that stir your soul and take your feelings to a deeper level. It took a few minutes, but eventually, I explained what I'm most passionate about."

I walked to the board, where I wrote as I recited, "My family.

"My faith.

"Staying healthy.

"Loving relationships.

"Work that satisfies me.

"Interests that excite and challenge me."

And, "Helping salespeople find their hidden potential and live a life of true happiness and success." I gestured to the list. "These are my passions."

Roger commented, "When you meet sales champions, you can see the passion in their eyes, hear it in their voices and feel it in their presence."

Luke Gaffney, Vice President of Sales, U.S. Corporate Markets, LexisNexis said: "If you don't have passion you can't win; at least not regularly. It's almost like an extra gear that is always available to kick in when you need it - and in sales, you need it often."

I continued, "Passion keeps you awake at night because you are excited about your goals and dreams. Passion motivates you to work on weekends and arrive to work before everyone else. Passion is what helps you get up after a bad fall and start all over."

Many people seem to believe that following their passion should be effortless. Unfortunately, it's not. It requires a lot of hard work, but the good news is that you'll enjoy it, because you're doing something you're excited about."

I drew a picture of a mountain with a snow-capped peak. "Rebecca Stephens was the first British woman to climb Mount Everest. Her climbing experience started when she was sent to Tibet by *The Financial Times* to write a story about climbers who were planning to scale the northeast ridge of Mount Everest. Prior to this journey, she knew nothing about mountain climbing, but the assignment had captured her attention and fueled her imagination.

"As she explained, 'What struck me most was that all the climbers had this passion to climb Everest. In every movement of their bodies, you could see how badly they wanted to conquer this mountain.'"

I panned a gaze across the room. "Have you ever seen an athlete have his or her greatest game with a take-it-or-leave-it attitude? Of course not! Passion is an essential ingredient to winning--from the basketball court to the boardroom. When people believe passionately in what they are doing and why they're doing it, they become unstoppable."

Key Principle # 40

Admit You're a Salesperson

We were now near the end of my training program, and I introduced the final principle, Principle Forty: Admit You're a Salesperson.

"If you sell for a living you have undoubtedly encountered society's viewpoint of the selling profession and of salespeople. What are the stereotypes of the salesman?"

Jenna Gomez answered, "Brash."

David McDonald added, "Exaggeration prone."

William Daniels said, "A fast-talking, slap-on-the-back type person."

I asked, "Do these descriptions accurately reflect the sales profession?" I wrote *NO* in big letters and underlined it. "Almost universally, people have preconceived notions of selling, including thoughts of unethical salespeople with little integrity. This belief, of course, is a misconception."

For many people, hearing the word "salesperson" sets off a chain reaction of negativity. Their mind sees a pushy guy with an avalanche of closing techniques ready to trap them into buying something they don't need or want.

It's definitely true that there are a lot of unprofessional salespeople. It is true that some can be pushy, manipulative, and aggressive. What is also true is that there are a lot of honest and authentic salespeople. Professionally-trained salespeople are well educated and empathetic individuals.

Professional salespeople forego short-term gain for long-term relationships. They know that if they're going to thrive in today's highly-competitive marketplace, they must always look after the best interests of their prospects and customers.

Sherman said, "The sales profession is a great profession. Salespeople must embrace a way of looking at their role that ensures they will not only be competent to perform the sales functions they have been entrusted with, but that they will conduct themselves with integrity as well."

I noted, "Without salespeople, our economy would slow to a crawl. Nothing happens until something is sold. Therefore, the selling profession is perhaps the most important economic asset to our society and economy.

"Selling pays the bills and keeps the doors open, but many salespeople are reluctant to admit to what they do. The sales fraternity doesn't want to be called 'salespeople' anymore. Salespeople wear 'masks' to disguise themselves and hide what they do for a living."

Misleading job titles such as account executive, market specialist, business development manager, consultant, regional manager, producer, marketing rep, and broker all facilitate this thinking. The funny thing is, you're a salesperson and you don't even know it.

Our culture may have created a negative perception of selling, but the truth is most of us engage in it every day, in nearly every professional and personal encounter in which we participate.

David raised his hand and spoke up. "Every company and every job today is dependent on the revenue generated from the selling of products and services as companies can no longer cut their way to profitability. The 'easy' money is gone from the landscape. Therefore, every member of every company has to do a better job building relationships, creating value and closing sales."

The front-line person who greets us at the door, answers the phone and directs us to the appropriate department. The customer service person who has now become both sales and service. The service department that manage the relationships after the sale. The principles of the company that are the face of the company and speak directly to customers. The accounting and purchasing departments that works with people on their bills and payments. They're all in sales!

While sales professionals lead the effort, internal and external customer contacts impact sales results at all levels. There is not a single person in an organization that does not have an opportunity to sell for their organization. Companies that focus on building customer loyalty through exceptional sales and customer service will win long term especially today.

I replied, "Excellent point. Robert Louis Stevenson, the great Scottish novelist said, 'Everyone lives by selling something.' Even if your job description doesn't have "sales" in it, you need to realize that you and everyone else are in sales from the moment the day starts. Be it convincing yourself that you're going to tackle a problem that's been looming; deciding between the chicken or shrimp salad; interacting with an irritated customer, or wooing others to your point of view, you are selling either to yourself or to someone else.

"Even highly trained professionals like lawyers and accountants need to land the next client. Some of you may earn money by providing consulting services--which by-the-way, must also be sold to the client--but the majority of you are salespeople who don't earn a dime until something is sold.

"Top performing salespeople take tremendous pride in the profession of selling and in themselves as human beings. They are proud, not only of what they do for a living, but also of the companies they work for and the products and services they sell."

I wrote *1., 2., 3.* on the board. "Now give three reasons you love being a salesperson."

When you're willing to admit that, indeed, you are actually in sales, you will appreciate how important it is to learn how to excel at it. Until you're able to say, "'I'm proud to be a salesperson,'" you are unconsciously creating a mental escape hatch that enables you to avoid being held accountable for your actions.

Acknowledging you are a professional salesperson will have a profound effect on your sales results. The negative emotional blockages will disappear, and you can kick your career into high gear and create a life for yourself and your family that is fulfilling and rewarding.

Key Lessons

- To get on the 'fast track' of success, determine the sales activities that are most important for achieving your goals and work on those activities first.

- Since there is always more work than time, setting priorities will help you manage your daily activities.

- Sales champions are never on vacation from their favorite pastime: the commitment to never-ending learning. Remember, there is always more to learn.

- What was good enough to get you where you are today will not be sufficient to get you to where you'll need to be in the future.

- If you are going to be successful, you have to give up the know-it-all attitude. Salespeople that suffer from 'know-it-all thinking' refuse to acknowledge that their thinking is the difference between them performing as an average salesperson as opposed to an extraordinary salesperson.

- People who act important are usually weak deep down inside. Their self-important attitude is a façade, intended to prevent you from seeing their weaknesses and to trick you into believing they're confident.

- It's important to enjoy what you're doing and believe in what you're selling.

- If you're selling halfheartedly, no amount of training or positive thinking can help you become a top performer. When people believe passionately in what they are doing and why they're doing it, they become unstoppable.

- Sales champions are passionate. They love their company and they exude this pride when talking about their products and services.

- The more passionate you are about your sales career, the greater the chances are that you will succeed.

- Don't forget that we're all in sales.

- Nothing happens until something is sold. Therefore, the selling profession is perhaps the most important economic asset to our society and economy.

- Until you're able to say, 'I'm proud to be a salesperson,' you are unconsciously creating a mental escape hatch that enables you to avoid being held accountable for your success.

Selling Skills *INSTITUTE*

Customized corporate on-site sales development programs
and peak performance sales coaching.
For information on the Selling Skills Institute's proprietary sales
development and individual peak performance sales coaching programs

Call us at:

339-927-2746

E-mail us at:

Charlie@shiftthinking.net

To order additional copies of
Shift Thinking, The Secret to Sales Greatness and Opportunity Calling
- The Easy Way to Double Your Number of New Appointments
Visit

sellingskillsinstitute.com

or

amazon.com